IMAGES
of America

DRY TORTUGAS
NATIONAL PARK

Perched in the Gulf of Mexico at the very end of Florida, Fort Jefferson is the cultural centerpiece of Dry Tortugas National Park. Reachable only by boat or seaplane, the park averages 60,000 visitors per year. This image from the late 1800s shows a young visitor among the fort's leftover Civil War–era cannonballs. (NPS.)

ON THE COVER: This 1890s image shows Public Health Service personnel in front of Fort Jefferson's sally port. At the time, the Dry Tortugas served as a quarantine station where ships inbound to the United States called for inspection and fumigation. Passengers and mariners were subject to quarantine as part of the national program to prevent contagious diseases, such as yellow fever and smallpox, from entering the United States. (NPS.)

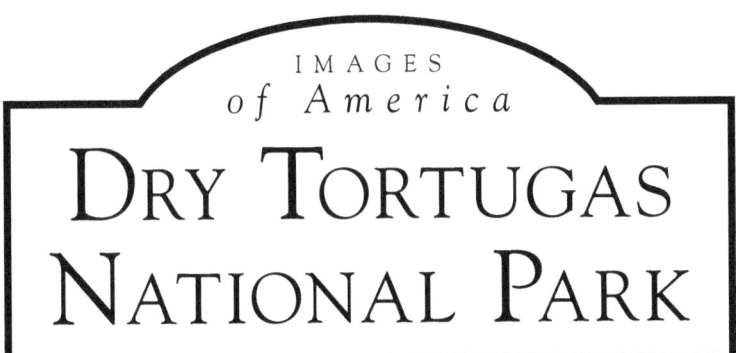
IMAGES of America
DRY TORTUGAS NATIONAL PARK

James A. Kushlan and Kirsten Hines

ARCADIA
PUBLISHING

Copyright © 2019 by James A. Kushlan and Kirsten Hines
ISBN 978-1-4671-0421-0

Published by Arcadia Publishing
Charleston, South Carolina

Library of Congress Control Number: 2019947303

For all general information, please contact Arcadia Publishing:
Telephone 843-853-2070
Fax 843-853-0044
E-mail sales@arcadiapublishing.com
For customer service and orders:
Toll-Free 1-888-313-2665

Visit us on the Internet at www.arcadiapublishing.com

Contents

Acknowledgments		6
Introduction		7
1.	Colonial Tortugas	11
2.	America's Southern Outpost	21
3.	The Civil War	47
4.	An American Backwater	69
5.	Birds and Reefs	87
6.	A Place Far Apart	101
Key to Courtesy Lines		127

Acknowledgments

This book pays tribute to the men and women of the National Park Service. That gratitude started personally in the late 1960s, when the senior author had the opportunity for over a decade to go to Fort Jefferson National Monument in the Dry Tortugas nearly annually, first as a graduate student and then as a National Park Service scientist. We thank current National Park Service staff who encouraged and advised us in writing this book: Everglades National Park superintendent Pedro Ramos, Dry Tortugas National Park manager Glenn Simpson, archivist Bonnie Ciolino and Courtney Christner of the South Florida Parks Collections Center, and cultural resource specialist Kelly Clark and archivist Nancy Russell, who kindly reviewed the book. We especially thank former park and Florida National Parks Association personnel Eloise and Chuck Pratt, who offered personal insights and their image collection. Former Dry Tortugas facility manager L. Wayne Landrum's book *Fort Jefferson and the Dry Tortugas National Park* remains an inspiration we highly recommend.

We thank boat captain Alex Allen and pilot Adam Schewitz of Key West Seaplane Adventures. At HistoryMiami Museum, we thank executive director Jorge Zamanillo, archive manager Ashley Trujillo, and collections assistant Kristen Lachterman. At the University of Miami, we thank Cristina Favretto and Nicola Hellman McFarland of the University of Miami Libraries Special Collections and Traci Ardren of the Department of Anthropology. We also thank Neill Wallis and Karen Walker of the Florida Museum of Natural History and Tina McDowell of the Carnegie Institution of Washington. At the Miami–Dade County Public Library, we thank Florida Collection librarian Giselle Alonso. At the Monroe County Public Library, we especially thank Monroe County historian Thomas Hambright for his guidance. Pioneer diver and underwater archeologist Robert F. Marx let us use one of his images. We thank Jane Tiedeman of the Key West Garden Club, the Ernest Hemingway Home and Museum, Key West Aquarium, Key West Art and Historical Society, Key West Shipwreck Museum, and the Mel Fisher Maritime Museum. And we thank the other historical repositories listed on page 127. At Arcadia Publishing, we thank our editors Stacia Bannerman and Liz Gurley.

Introduction

The islands of the Dry Tortugas arise "as if by magic floating on top of the Gulf waters." This is how Dr. Joseph Bassett Holder described where he and his family lived during the American Civil War, the moment of the Dry Tortugas' greatest fame and also infamy. The sandy islets and the massive Fort Jefferson, lying at the nexus of critical sea lanes, do indeed appear out of nowhere to a boat approaching from the Gulf of Mexico, the Atlantic Ocean, mainland Florida, or Cuba. These islands and the tropical reefs and shallows around them are the stuff of novels and adventure stories, pirates and navies, war and peace, hardship and tranquility. The Dry Tortugas remain today remote, historic, and pristine: remote, as the westernmost outpost of the Florida Keys, 68 miles west of Key West and only roughly 110 miles north of Havana; historic, bearing the second-oldest persistent place name in all of North America and the location of America's most ambitious coastal fortification; and pristine, with coral reefs that are among the most intact in the Florida Keys and Caribbean and seabird colonies unique within North America. Its remoteness, history, and environment are now protected in perpetuity within Dry Tortugas National Park.

Geologically, the islands of the Dry Tortugas are the last bits of land at the southwest tip of the Florida platform, beyond which the seafloor falls away to abyssal depths. About 18,000 years ago, with sea levels over 300 feet lower than at present, what are now the islands of the Dry Tortugas and surrounding Tortugas Bank were dry land, part of a then much larger Florida peninsula. As sea level rose, the land submerged, and the Tortugas' islands formed on slight topographic highs atop ancient coral reefs. In contrast, the Marquesas and Florida Keys to the east are perched atop sedimentary limestone. The elliptical Tortugas reef track surrounds a lagoon of seagrass, sand, and rock bottom punctuated by the Tortugas' few islands. The islands, known as keys, are accumulations of current- and storm-borne locally derived sand and broken bits of coral. At present, the total land area is about 100 acres; the national park covers about 100 square miles, so only 0.15 percent of the park is land.

The islands change. As this is written, there are five, as several connected in recent decades. A future storm may separate them again. To a visitor, the keys still go by seven names, Bush, Garden, East, Hospital, Loggerhead, Long, and Middle. Loggerhead Key is the highest naturally and largest at 64 acres. Garden Key is nearly covered with Fort Jefferson. The other keys' locations, sizes, shapes, and existence over time have been altered by storms and currents, as well as by dredging the harbor and mining their sand and coral rubble. There were 11 islands in 1513 and again in 1773, when they were first officially charted. Their names changed and interchanged over time. The current Garden Key was initially charted as Bush Key. Current Bush Key, where the terns nest, was called Long Key and vice versa. East and Middle Keys have kept their names, although Middle was first charted as Bird Key. Loggerhead Key has had a consistent history, initially being charted as Logger Head Turtle Key, and likely was the one that impressed Ponce de León and for which he named Tortuga. Hospital Key was previously named Middle Key and Sand Key. The original Southwest, North, and Northeast Keys disappeared by 1875, and Bird Key, after suffering years of erosion, disappeared in the 1930s. Much of Long and Bush Keys' sand was used to build the fort. North Key Harbor, Bird Key Bank, and Bird Key Harbor recall disappeared islands. The smaller keys submerged seasonally or in storms; sandbanks periodically emerged. Eleven major hurricanes are documented to have impacted the Dry Tortugas, clearly a place where unpredictable, sometimes violent, natural forces still determine the landscape.

South Florida's indigenous peoples, who occupied villages on the Keys and mainland, knew of the Tortugas, as it was captive Gulf Coast Indians who led Juan Ponce de León there in 1513. In the over 500 years since their European "discovery," the Tortugas' historical roles have proven diverse and evolving but always linked to the surrounding seas. The Tortugas Bank abuts the deep waters of the Florida Strait, which serves as a direct 110-mile-long east-west passageway between the Gulf and the Atlantic. After Ponce de León, for most of the next three centuries, the Tortugas, like all of peninsular Florida, were a Spanish possession. Lying directly north of Havana, they were a waypoint for Spanish ships coming from Cuba and for those who would prey on them. The Florida Strait provided an essential passageway for navies, ships of commerce, pirates and privateers, fishermen, and refugees. As the Loop Current of the Gulf of Mexico passes the Tortugas and enters the strait, it becomes the Florida Current, which flows eastwards and then northwards along fringing reefs and shoals. This was one of the world's more dangerous passageways, claiming thousands of ships from many nations for half a millennium. Given their navigational importance at the western head of the strait, "Tortugas," and later "Tortugas Secas," were a prominent feature of historic navigation charts and well known to centuries of mariners.

Through their Spanish history, the Tortugas were tied to the nearest city and port: Havana. From Cuba came mariners to catch fish, hunt turtles, and gather turtle and seabird eggs for the Havana market. For over two centuries, 1566 to 1790, the Flota de Indias, or the Spanish plate fleet, sailed periodically from Havana. This convoy carried the goods of the Spanish empire back to the motherland and was the source of Spain's wealth and, therefore, its military and political power. The fleet embarked in Havana and headed to catch the eastward flow of the Florida Current off the Tortugas.

Ships following this route had to navigate its dangers. Southwest Reef near Loggerhead Key was a primary grounding spot for sailing vessels attempting to pass the Tortugas, particularly in storms or at night. North winds drove ships onto the Tortugas' northern reefs. Ships cutting through the Rebecca Channel wrecked on its bank and East Key. Ships continuing eastwards in the strait next encountered the extensive shoals called the Quicksands, then the shallows of the Marquesas, and finally the coral reefs that reappear at Key West and offshore following the alignment of the Florida Keys. These sailing ships had to contend with the powerful Florida Current running west to east while sailing head-on into the prevailing easterly wind. And they had to contend with unpredictable westerly flowing counter-currents and even more unpredictable eddies. The wind in the strait might die totally, quickly clock around due to transient frontal systems from the north, or turn into a tropical hurricane. Storms such as those in 1622, 1715, 1733, and 1750 caused Flota ships to wreck on the shallows, some on or near the Tortugas.

The enterprise of salvaging wrecked ships began as soon as such ships started sailing past the reefs. Indians quickly took to the wrecking art, the plunder from which just as quickly began altering their pre-contact civilization. Spain stationed wreckers in Havana to recover much of what was lost. But ships of all sorts and from many seafaring nations came to grief on the shallows, eventually creating a wrecking economy along the Florida coast in which rescued ships and goods were sold by Bahamian or Cuban salvors in Havana, Nassau, or St. Augustine and later by Americans in Key West. Bahamians were wrecking on the keys as early as the 1730s and increased their presence when Florida Keys Indians hostile to them departed with the Spanish. By the early 1800s, wrecking was the primary income for the government in Nassau. Wreckers worked the reefs off the Tortugas and to the east throughout the age of sailing ships.

The colonial era was intermittently a time of pirates and privateers in the Florida Strait, usually called the New Bahama Channel. The Dry Tortugas were a stopping point, but there likely was never a permanent settlement given the smallish islands and lack of fresh water. In nearby Cuba and the Bahamas, the situation at times was quite different. In the early 1700s, Nassau was run by pirates, and from Cuba's Matanzas Bay, pirates and privateers could access the southern side of the strait. From the Tortugas, both privateers and official navies could wait watchfully along the strait's northern border.

It was only after Spain turned Florida over to the United States in 1821 that the Dry Tortugas became more than a fishing, provisioning, rendezvous, and stopping-over place. Their strategic position was not lost on their new government, and the Tortugas were quickly claimed, reconnoitered, and identified as a place needing a lighthouse and a fort. The first lighthouse was built on what is now Garden Key in 1825–1826. It was supplemented by a taller tower closer to the reefs on Loggerhead Key in 1858. Construction of the massive Fort Jefferson started in 1846. It was to become America's most ambitious and extensive permanent coastal fortification, requiring an estimated 16 million bricks, each one shipped in from distant brickyards. In some shipments, over two-thirds were found to be deficient.

The fort was designed and constructed by some of the most notable engineers of the era and represented the pinnacle of permanent fortifications, with tower bastions, detached scarps, and gun ports with protective shutters to increase its firepower. It was designed to achieve a maximum range of fire to protect itself and nearby anchorages from attack. It also was designed such that a thousand soldiers could withstand a yearlong siege.

Once the Tortugas became part of the United States, their history became inexorably tied to that of Key West, South Florida's first town. A civilian settlement was founded on Cayo Hueso immediately after Florida's cession to the United States so as to take advantage of its natural harbor and wrecking opportunities nearby. Among the government's first tasks were to deploy a revenue fleet to patrol the strait and to establish a home port for the United States' West Indian Squadron, charged with ending piracy and slave running. The Tortugas were rejected for this role in favor of Key West, but their harbors were used by the fleet as well as wreckers, fishermen, and eggers. Key West became a port of entry in 1822. When Bahamian wreckers working the keys were no longer allowed to take their salvage to Nassau, and a court with admiralty powers was established in Key West, Bahamians moved to the keys, becoming "Conchs." Key West grew and prospered, its economy underpinned not only by wrecking and its harbor but also by salt production, fisheries, military spending, and a growing population. Coincident with the building of Fort Jefferson was the construction of Fort Taylor in Key West. The Dry Tortugas were Key West's western outpost, commercially and militarily.

As they had marked the Spanish sea lanes, the Dry Tortugas were called upon to secure critical American commerce coming from the Mississippi River. And they also served to project American defensive and offensive postures toward new countries and remaining European colonies to the west and south and to support the blockade of the Confederacy in the Civil War. During the war, the fort was armed and garrisoned and played an additional role as a military prison. The military prisoners' hard labor was used to continue construction. Other prisoners famously included those convicted of complicity in the assassination of Abraham Lincoln. Of these, Dr. Samuel Mudd remains the most persistently famous. Notoriety ensued, as prisoners, especially the convicted Conspirators, complained of conditions in letters that reached newspapers, Congress, and the president. Indeed, isolation, poor sanitation, dense population, and persistent supply difficulties made for challenging conditions. The Tortugas became known as America's Devil's Island.

After the Civil War, with lighthouses installed on the reefs themselves, accurate charts, transportation alternatives by railroad, better navigation, and better steerage offered by screw propellers and steam power, wrecks and the wrecking business declined. The economy of the lower keys diversified with cigar making, turtling, sponging, island agriculture, and shipping. By 1890, Key West was the largest city in Florida. The Overseas Railroad arrived in 1912, opening Key West and nearby Dry Tortugas to the world.

On the Dry Tortugas after the Civil War, the fort was initially modernized, new armaments brought in, and construction continued in spurts depending on funding and strategy. Intermittently, the Dry Tortugas saw service as a quarantine station for America-bound ships, a naval reservation, a navigational aid depot, and a coal and water resupply station. It was from the Dry Tortugas that the battleship *Maine* left for Havana Harbor and played her role as the ignition point for the Spanish-American War. In subsequent wars, the Dry Tortugas served as an observational and communications outpost and seaplane base. Unofficially, the Tortugas continued to attract sightseers and fishermen, both sport and commercial, mostly from Key West. Presidents, authors, and adventuresome tourists visited.

Eventually, the fort was left unfinished. Such forts came to be considered indefensible from rifled cannon shot, and the job of defending the Florida Strait fell to the mobile Navy. Following a hurricane and yellow fever outbreak, the US Army withdrew from the fort in 1874, and with lack of maintenance, the masonry work began to deteriorate, as any structure exposed to the marine environment and tropical storms would. Its mortar was made from local salty sand dug out of the beaches. Rain seeped through the roof and around the bricks. Hurricanes ravished buildings; fires burned wooden structures and weakened walls.

As intriguing as the Dry Tortugas' human history is, so is the story of its natural resources. It was the biological (or at least edible) resources of the Tortugas that impressed Ponce de León. Thereafter for centuries, provisioning mariners and commercial harvesters came to the Dry Tortugas, although leaving little trace. Sea turtles and their eggs, seabirds and their eggs, and fish found their way into ships' stores or to the markets in Havana and Key West. In 1850 and 1851, Louis Agassiz scientifically studied the Tortugas' reefs, studies taken up by his mentee Joseph Bassett Holder, quoted in the opening line of this introduction. Research expeditions also came in 1869, 1877–1878, 1885, and 1902. In 1878, a "black-water" event killed marine life, increasing interest in research. From 1904 to 1939, the Tortugas Laboratory of the Carnegie Institution of Washington operated a marine research station on Loggerhead Key. Many of the great natural scientists of the era came to study. The Tortugas' marine life became among the best documented in the world, recorded in hundreds of scientific papers.

In spring and summer, sea turtles nested on the beaches. Sharks and other fish used the shallows as breeding and nursery areas. Marlin and other pelagic fish traveled the Florida Strait. Many species of birds migrating from their wintering grounds descended on the islands. Seabird species bred on the Dry Tortugas that nested nowhere else in the continental United States. The seabirds brought the Dry Tortugas to the attention of Pres. Theodore Roosevelt, who, in 1908, declared the nesting islands a bird reserve so as to offer protection from egg harvest. Under the watchful eyes of wardens, the colonies thrived. In 1935, Pres. Franklin Roosevelt, who had visited the islands previously, declared Fort Jefferson a national monument, and the degree of government protection increased.

The national monument designation focused on historic Fort Jefferson. In 1980, the monument incorporated 73 square miles of waters. The monument area was enlarged by Congress in 1983. In 1992, it was redesignated as Dry Tortugas National Park. The park protected the historic structures, shipwrecks, islands, reefs, and shallows. Incorporating both historic Fort Jefferson and critical marine natural areas, the park aspired to protect its nationally significant scenic, cultural, marine, and scientific values for the education and inspiration of the public. Consumptive use became managed for the benefit of the resources, and all artifacts were protected above and below water. Little by little, the fort was stabilized and restored. Visitors, averaging over 60,000 a year, came to Dry Tortugas National Park, despite its being accessible only by boat or seaplane. The islands of Dry Tortugas National Park still arise as if by magic from the waters, surrounded by untrammeled coral reefs and sandy shallows.

One
COLONIAL TORTUGAS

Although the unstable sands of the Dry Tortugas precluded persistence of artifacts, Native Americans who lived in the region knew of the islands. For Juan Ponce de León, the Tortugas proved a remarkable provisioning site. Ponce de León generally created place names with religious connotations, but here, he was impressed by the abundance of turtles on a nesting island he called simply "Tortuga." The name stuck. Following Ponce de León, the Spanish governments in St. Augustine and Havana showed no particular interest in the keys, which they called Las Martires, other than assuring the fate of Spanish ships that wrecked nearby. For this they engaged ever-decreasing local populations of Native Americans to provide notification, to help salvage, and to not kill or enslave castaway Spanish seamen and passengers.

There was no permanent Spanish settlement on the Tortugas, but the islands served as a critical landmark. With little effective governmental control, pirates, privateers, and naval ships of various nations made use of the security of the Dry Tortugas' harbors to hide out, repair ships, escape storms, or await passing opportunities. Spanish fishermen visited the Keys and Gulf Coast to supply the Havana market, establishing fishing settlements called ranchos on Key West and elsewhere. The most profitable enterprise of the late colonial period was wrecking by Cuban Spanish and Bahamians. The Dry Tortugas were a welcoming harbor from which to await wrecks that, with some regularity, piled into their nearby reefs, at times immediately in front of the islands. When Spain turned Florida over to the British in 1763 and Spanish and remnant Indians left, South Florida was emptied of people. With the change in government, surveying to support settlement and commerce became a priority, and the Dry Tortugas were, for the first time, accurately charted. During the second period of Spanish rule, nearly 40 years starting in 1783, the Dry Tortugas and the nearby keys continued to accommodate Bahamian and Cuban wreckers, fishermen, and woodcutters, and Spain awarded land grants in the Florida Keys, although no settlements followed.

Native Americans dwelled in the lower Florida Keys for thousands of years and continued to do so through the Spanish colonial period. Over 150 habitation sites have been documented through the Keys, including Key West. The Indians, generally called Matecumbe by the 16th-century Spanish, were a distinct group of an advanced hunter-gatherer culture utilizing the abundant marine and upland island resources, as shown by these artifacts of pottery and shell tools from Stock Island. Using long wooden canoes, they were accomplished mariners, and by the late 1500s, they had learned from the Spanish to sail small boats to Havana. Keys Indians quickly became skilled at wrecking and over the centuries became increasingly inculcated with aspects of the dominant Spanish culture. By the early 1700s, it became policy to resettle Florida Keys Indians to Cuba. It was reported by Bernard Romans that, anticipating the English accession of Florida, the Indians left the Keys before and when the Spanish withdrew. (UMA.)

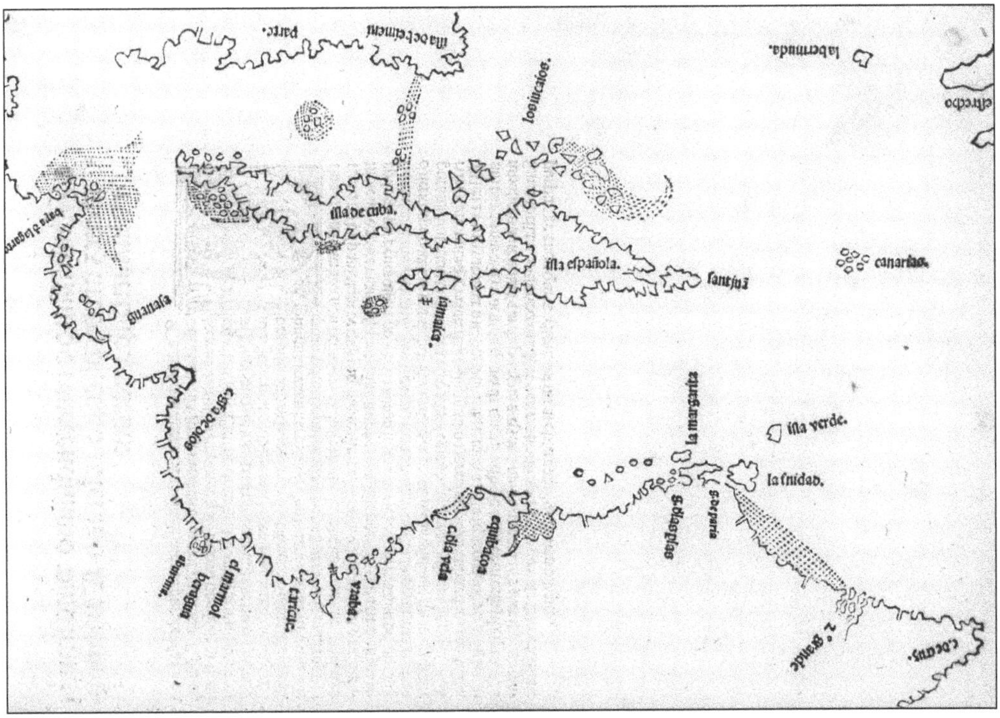

The existence of land north of Cuba was known soon after Columbus's first voyage. This 1511 map from Pietro Martire d'Anghiera shows islands in the formation and location of the Dry Tortugas. Florida had been surreptitiously visited by Spanish expeditions before Juan Ponce de León's official voyage, in which he encountered at least one Indian who could speak some Spanish, and the Calusa were already hostile to the Spanish. (JCBL.)

Rounding the keys, Ponce de León took a northbound course to the mainland, likely using Rebecca Channel, leaving the Tortugas to his west. On his return trip, he found the islands on June 21, 1513. It was a useful provisioning stop, yielding 170 sea turtles, 5,000 seabirds, and 14 now-extinct monk seals (shown). Turtles, kept alive aboard ship until butchered, were highly desirable food for protein-hungry mariners. (NOAA.)

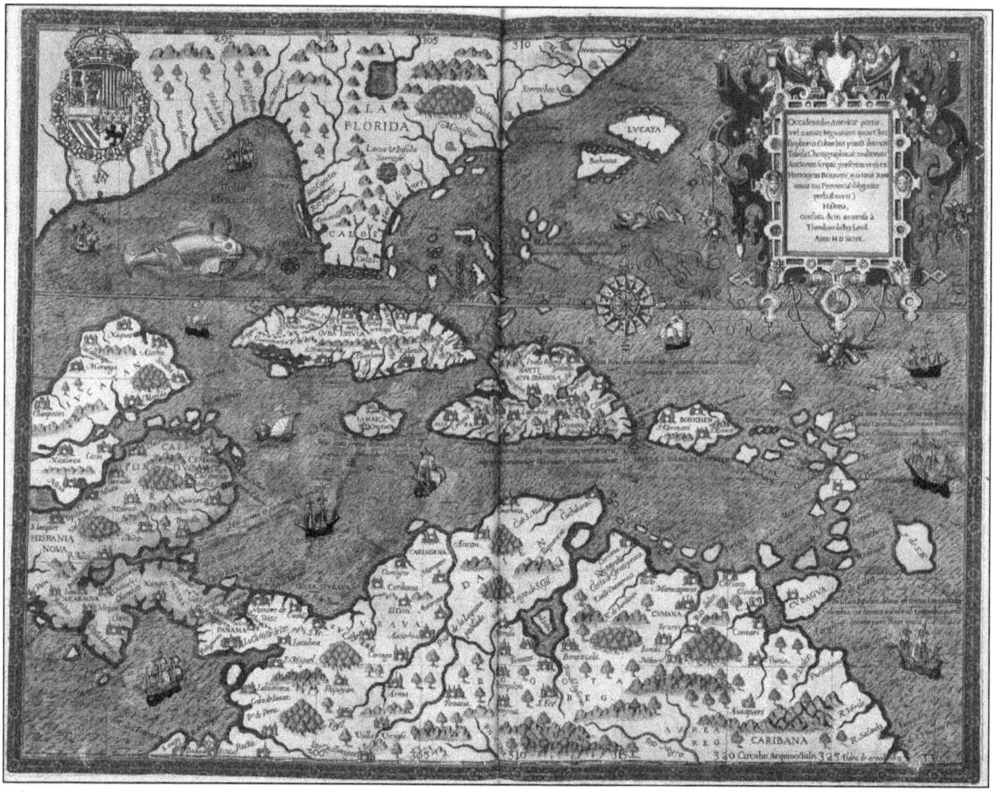

The Tortugas appeared on navigation charts, initially as Tortuga. In this 1594 chart, they are Insulæ dictæ Testudines, Islands of the Turtles. They became Tortugas Secas in Spanish, or "Dry Tortugas." The name is often attributed to there being no fresh water. However, mariners would not expect fresh water there. It is more likely information that the place called "turtles" in the middle of the ocean had "dry" (*seca*) land. (JCBL.)

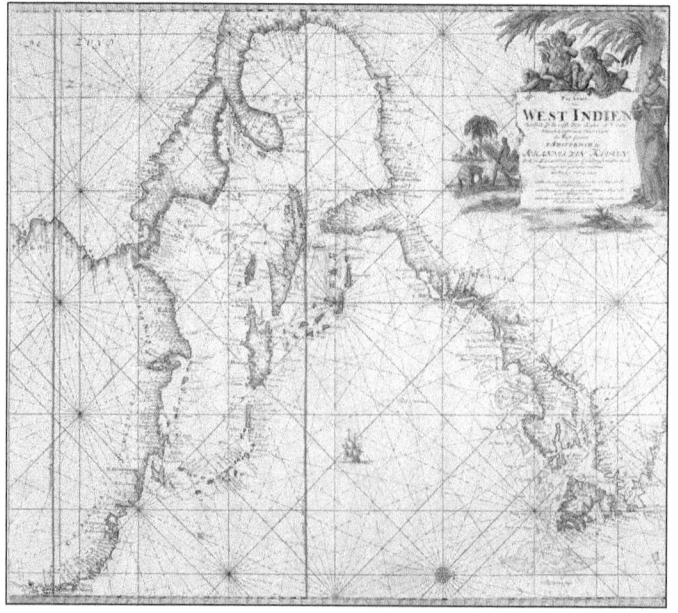

The Dry Tortugas served landmark and anchorage roles throughout the colonial period. This late-1600s chart is oriented in the direction that ships from Europe would travel. The Florida Strait is the most direct passage through the lands lined up from Florida through the Antilles to Havana, the Gulf of Mexico, and New Spain (Mexico). (NYPL.)

Of greatest importance to colonial Spain was the periodic sailing of its transport fleet, the Flota de Indias. For over two centuries, the fleet carried goods and products, such as precious metals, gems, and pearls, from the New World to Spain. The king's 20 percent cut funded the government and its wars. The fleet assembled in Havana and then headed northward, catching the Florida Current just off the Dry Tortugas. Safe from attack owing to the number of ships traveling together, the Flota's passage generally went well. But in September 1622, departing Havana six weeks late and well into the hurricane season, the fleet wrecked in a storm. The *Santa Margarita* went down near the Marquesas and *Nuestra Señora Rosario* off the Tortugas; both were soon partially salvaged. *Nuestra Señora de Atocha* sank between the Tortugas and the Marquesas. The *Atocha*'s debris was spread by a subsequent storm, and in 55 feet of water, its cargo of Colombian gold, Peruvian and Mexican silver, copper, pearls, emeralds, and indigo was out of reach of colonial salvors. The fleet's wreck was an economic blow to Spain. (RM.)

The colonial era was a time of piracy, privateering, and naval warfare around the Tortugas. Pirates robbed ships illegally; privateers did so legally, being authorized by governments to attack enemies of the moment. Off the Tortugas, passage was constricted, and traffic volume was high. English privateer and organizer of the Royal Navy Sir John Hawkins (shown) stopped at the Dry Tortugas in 1565 to provision with turtles and seabirds. (NMML.)

Piracy proliferated when wars ended and privateering was deauthorized, peaking from the mid-1600s to 1720s and again after the end of the War of 1812. During the golden age of pirates in the 1600s, they famously based themselves at Tortuga (shown), which was not the Dry Tortugas but a turtle-shaped island off Hispaniola. From 1706 to 1718, Nassau served as a pirate capital convenient to work the Florida Strait. (UTL.)

The Dry Tortugas were certainly a station for pirates. Robert Lewis Stevenson, in his 1880 novel *Treasure Island*, offered his fictionalized account of Billy Bones's dreadful stories "about hanging, and walking the plank, and storms at sea, and the Dry Tortugas." One of its illustrations is shown. Such use was confirmed in the mid-1900s, when a lighthouse keeper uncovered Spanish silver there. (Illustration by N.C. Wyeth, UCL.)

One of the more consequential engagements in colonial Caribbean history occurred off the Tortugas, where privateer fleets habitually assembled. In 1628, Dutch admiral Piet Pieterszoon Heyn (shown) waited near the Tortugas for the Spanish Flota's departure from Havana. When the wind died, the Dutch ships drifted to Matanzas Bay, trapping a 17-ship treasure fleet. The Spanish government went bankrupt, the Netherlands gained their independence, and Heyn became a national hero. (NM.)

17

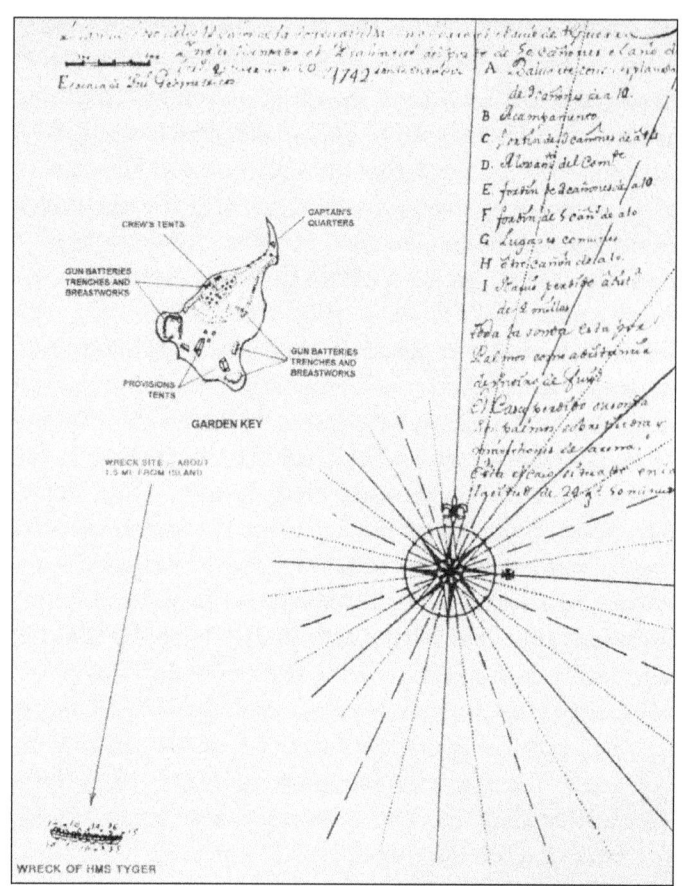

WRECK OF HMS TYGER

The Tortugas shallows continued to take ships throughout the colonial period. In 1742, while patrolling off Cuba, the distinguished hundred-year-old British ship HMS *Tyger* ran aground on the Tortugas' reefs. The crew built the Dry Tortugas' first fortification (shown), a stockade where they avoided Spanish capture for 56 days. On a reconditioned wrecked sloop and their own small boats, the castaways eventually made it to Port Royal, Jamaica, 700 miles away. (KH.)

To work wrecked ships along the Florida reef, Spain used trained crews from Havana, employing Florida Indians and slaves as divers. Later, private wreckers came from Cuba and the Bahamas. When not attending to vessels in distress, wrecker crews also caught fish, hunted turtles, collected bird eggs, cut fine lumber, or made charcoal for the Nassau or Havana markets. (SLAF.)

Between 1763 and 1783, when Florida's colonial ownership had transferred to Great Britain, the Dry Tortugas were finally properly surveyed. George Gauld's work in 1773 provided detailed depth and location information for the Tortugas waters and gave names to the existing islands. The Tortugas portion of his map is shown. Gauld's charts were praised for their accuracy for decades after and were a baseline for the area. (USNA.)

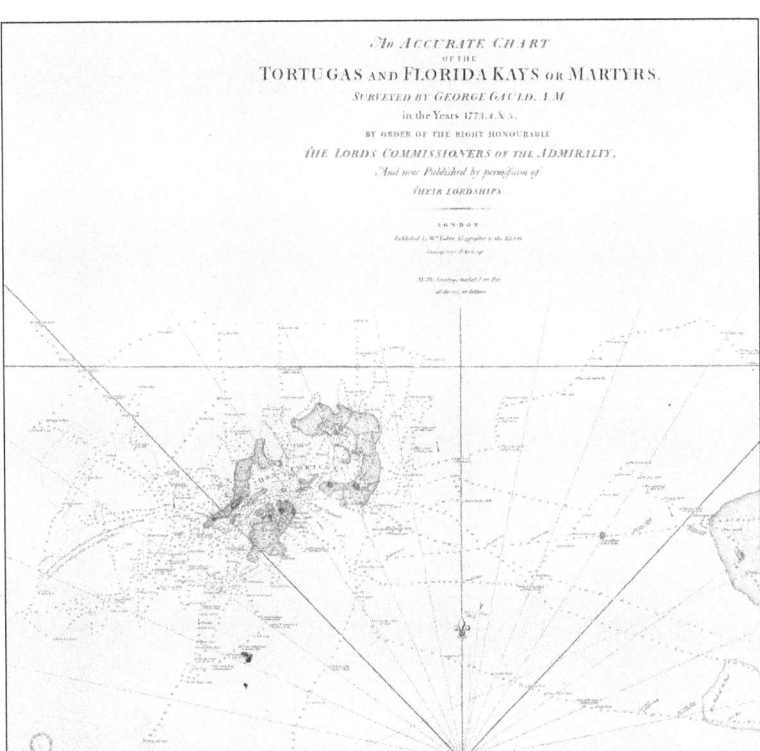

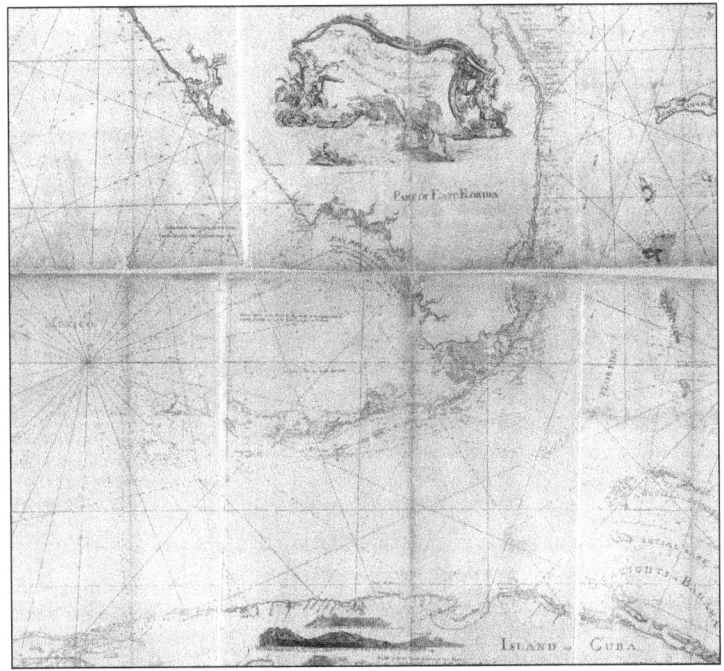

Surveyor and naturalist Bernard Romans first encountered the Tortugas in 1766, when his personal sloop *Mary* ran aground there. His later survey of the Dry Tortugas fed into his broader reconnaissance of the coasts of South Florida, Cuba, and the Gulf of Mexico. Romans famously published his observations on piloting the coast, natural history, and botany in 1775. This chart of his was published in 1781. (LOC.)

The British hold on Florida lasted only 20 years. After the American Revolution, in 1783, Florida was transferred back to Spain, which retained it for nearly 40 more years. Unlike during its previous tenure, Spain encouraged settlement and awarded land grants in South Florida. In 1815, the Havana-based captain-general of Cuba and Florida, Juan Ruiz de Apodaca (shown), awarded a land grant of the island of Cayo Hueso to a naval officer, Juan Pablo Salas, making him the first proprietor of Key West. Salas, however, did not choose to settle there. Florida proved a burden to Spain, which was unable to withstand American assaults within its territory that were targeting Indians and slaves who had escaped to Spanish Florida and otherwise were destabilizing Spanish control. The Dry Tortugas' colonial era ended in 1821, when Spain deeded Florida over to the United States. (SBS.)

Two

America's Southern Outpost

The strategic opportunities of the Florida Keys were immediately appreciated by the US government. On March 25, 1822, Lt. Commander Matthew C. Perry planted the American flag on Key West to assure that American ownership of this remote island had passed to the United States and was not being retained by Spain. He named it Thomson's Island; the name never took. Perry then sailed to the Dry Tortugas, where he established American sovereignty on this even more remote piece of deserted land, confirmed its strategic importance, and recommended building a lighthouse.

Even before Perry's visit, lured by its harbor and location, Cayo Hueso had come to the attention of American commercial interests. Juan Salas contracted to trade his island to John B. Strong, who then transferred his rights to John Geddes. In January 1822, Salas also sold the island to New Orleans businessman John W. Simonton. Geddes arranged to take possession of the island in April 1822, but with Salas eventually making reparations, Simonton and his partners' claim prevailed. Mariners, settlers, and businessmen moved in from the north. Less than a two-day sail from the Tortugas, a town and seaport took shape.

Simonton lobbied Washington for a military base, and in 1822, Capt. David Porter arrived to establish a homeport for his West Indian anti-pirate operations and, as he felt authorized, to take military control of Key West—a move not appreciated by the civilian proprietors. In 1824, construction of the Tortugas' first lighthouse began. In 1845, Garden Key was proclaimed a military reservation by James K. Polk. In December 1846, work began building a fort there. Government interest in the Tortugas had derived in large part from the need to protect expanding trade routes from the Mississippi River and Gulf Coast. In 1850, the fort was named after the Louisiana Purchase's architect, Thomas Jefferson. The 1850s also brought scientific attention to the Dry Tortugas with state-of-the-art navigational and biological surveys. As the Civil War approached, Federal construction of the fort by Army engineers continued using seasonal Northern workers and slaves rented from Key West owners.

Nearly two decades before the Dry Tortugas became part of the United States, the Louisiana Purchase of 1803 foreshadowed their importance. The acquisition opened the center of the continent to agriculture, connected to the rest of the United States through Mississippi River shipping, which passed the Tortugas, as did shipping from Mexico, Central America, and Cuba. The Tortugas were seen as a vital asset by the American federal government. (USNA.)

Matthew Perry's reconnaissance of Florida's coastline confirmed not only the Tortugas' strategic importance but also the dangers posed by the reefs and shallows nearby. His recommendations for lighthouses included Key Biscayne, Key Largo, off Key West, and on Southwest Key in the Tortugas. The plan and funding were soon approved by Congress, and work began on all four lights. The recommended sites were shifted on Key West and the Tortugas. (MMA.)

After the War of 1812, out-of-work privateers took to piracy. In 1822, Capt. David Porter received command of the United States' first multi-ship taskforce, the West Indies Squadron of 17 ships, including the Navy's first steam-powered vessel. From Key West, the 1,000-man squadron successfully pursued pirates, especially along the Cuban coast south of the Dry Tortugas. This image depicts the assembled fleet in Key West Harbor in 1823. (MCPL.)

Porter selected Key West for his base over the Tortugas, which he found wholly inadequate. This 1826 drawing is the view from the commandant's porch by Philadelphia naturalist Titian Peale. Key West prospered from its strategic location along the shipping lane. By 1829, a town was platted, and with piracy under control, the harbor, wrecking, salt production, fishing, and increasing population also emerged as economic drivers for the region. (MCPL.)

With the Navy off fighting Caribbean pirates, the Treasury Department's Revenue Cutter Service was the US government's primary border patrol in the Tortugas. The Charleston-based *Marion* called as early as 1826. The USRC *Gallatin* is shown. The service enforced customs and tonnage duties, a main source of income for the federal government at the time. With broad authority, the Revenue Service conducted regular patrols to the Dry Tortugas. (NHHC.)

The first Tortugas lighthouse, 70 feet tall and built on the inner harbor, was first lit on July 4, 1826. By the arrival of the second keeper, Joseph Himinez, the next year, a ship had already wrecked because of a blind spot in its light field. Being early in the history of photography, there are no photographs known of the stand-alone light; this one shows the lighthouse with the fort around it. (NPS.)

The ship traffic passing by the Tortugas was heavy. In 1822, Key West was made a port of entry. In 1828, over 200 ships entered the port, and in one year, nearly 50 ships were reported to have wrecked on the reefs. Bahamian and New England wreckers patrolled and waited on station along the reef, anchoring in harbors such as at the Dry Tortugas. (MCPL.)

The wintering New Englanders and territorial government wanted Bahamian wreckers gone, so in 1825, Congress required salvage be brought to an American port of entry. In 1828, James Webb (shown) was appointed the first judge of a federal court in Key West having admiralty jurisdiction. Successor William Marvin wrote the book on wrecking law. Wrecking made money for everyone—wreckers, warehouse owners, dockhands, agents, lawyers, shippers, and crooked captains. (MCPL.)

For over 20 years, the lighthouse keepers and families were solitary residents in the Dry Tortugas. James Fenimore Cooper's novel *Jack Tier or the Florida Reef Tract*, in 1848 and its earlier serialization, brought a minor degree of literary fame to the early lighthouse, which was one of the story's settings. Wrecks continued as the light dimmed further, in part because smoke from inferior oil fogged its reflectors. (MDCPL.)

In 1832, the USRC *Marion* brought naturalist John James Audubon to draw for his *Birds of America*. Audubon was able to see birds he found nowhere else in America. Today in Key West, Audubon's visit is commemorated by the Audubon House & Tropical Gardens, built in 1846 by wrecker John Geiger. The Geiger tree in Audubon's white-crowned pigeon plate (shown) is named for him. (Painting by J.J. Audubon, RP.)

With the lighthouse in place, attention turned to defense. In 1829, Lt. Joseph Tattnall (shown) and G.R. Gednery surveyed the Tortugas, reporting that multiple ships could anchor in the outer harbor, while the inner harbor was protected by a narrow entrance. He advised that a hostile power occupying the Tortugas would put American shipping in peril and recommended a fort to protect these anchorages and thwart foreign powers. (NHHC.)

The policy to erect permanent coastal fortifications resulted from America's failure to secure unfortified Washington during the War of 1812 contrasted with the successful defense of Baltimore. Joseph Gilbert Totten (shown) became chair of the fortifications board and chief of the Army engineers, and he also cofounded the National Academy of Sciences. He guided the strategy from 1838 to 1864. Construction on the Dry Tortugas' fort began in 1846. (LOC.)

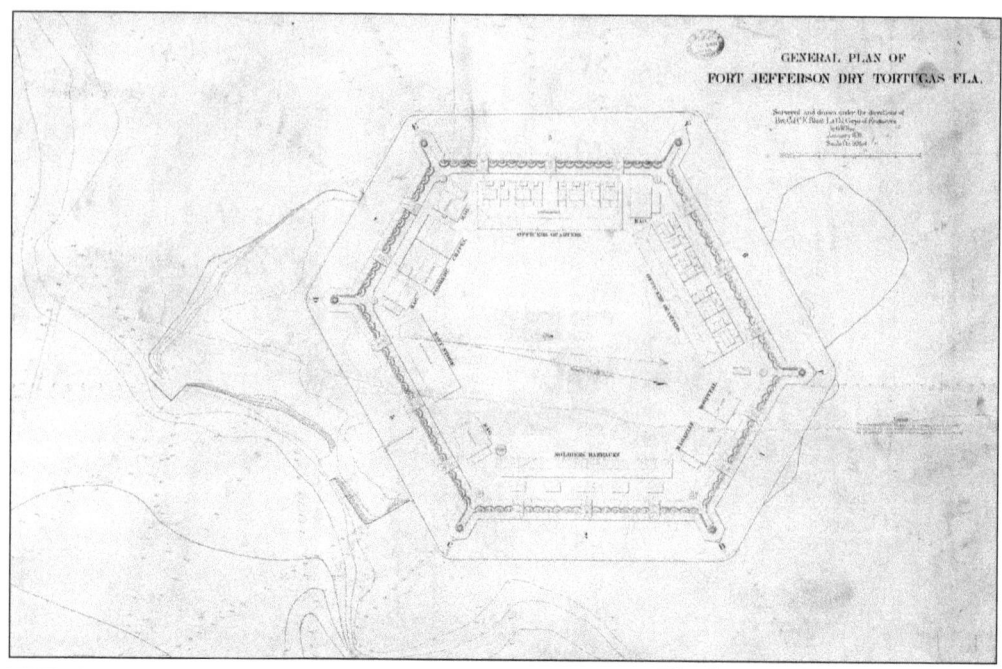

The fort was designed by Totten and Montgomery C. Meigs. Unlike sister Third System forts designed for intermittent manning, Fort Jefferson was uniquely anticipated to house a permanent contingent of hundreds of Regular Army troops, armaments, and supplies. Two years after the fort's construction was begun, Totten's subordinate Robert E. Lee, surveying farther north, named islands for Totten and Meigs in what is now Biscayne National Park. (USNA.)

Horatio Wright was in charge of the fort's construction from 1846 to 1856, as was Daniel Phineas Woodbury (shown), from 1856 to 1861. Wright was an expert on ironwork and Woodbury on fort architecture. Woodbury wrote a book called *Sustaining Walls*. In 1863, he returned as commandant of Key West and the Tortugas but died of yellow fever in Key West. Wright became chief of engineers in 1884. (LOC.)

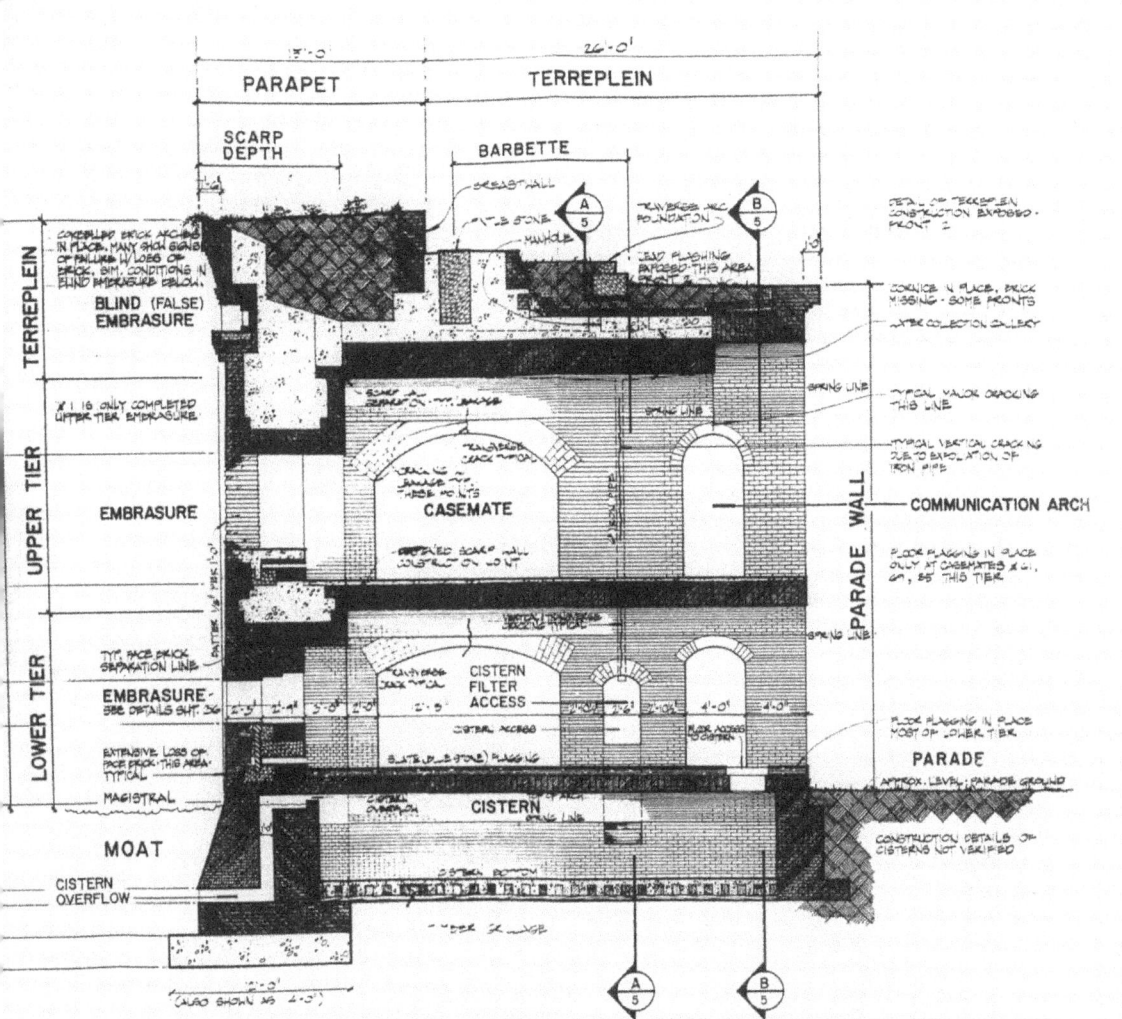

This image shows a cross-section and vocabulary of the fort, which called for a two-story outer curtain wall, or scarp, behind which were two tiers of double-arched interconnecting gun rooms, called casemates, in which cannon were to be mounted. Toward the interior, smaller communication arches created a passageway between casemates. Each casemate had an exterior opening, called an embrasure, for a cannon to fire outwards. The third tier had false, or blind, embrasures giving the impression of more cannon. The outward-facing parapet held small rooms into which gunners could retreat. Behind was the barbette holding a top row of cannon. The rest of the roof was a sand-filled terreplein through which rainwater could filter and be channeled down to cisterns beneath the fort. The water channel was accessible on the lower tier through an arch between the casemate arches and the communication arch. On the exterior, the structure was to be bounded by a moat, and the interior was a large open space called the parade. (NPS.)

Fort Jefferson is one of the most ambitious of the masonry forts in the United States. Early bricks failed to withstand the climate and were replaced by those sourced from Pensacola, which were larger and more orange. During the Civil War, with Southern brick unavailable, Northern brick was again used towards the top of the fort. The different size and color of bricks used over the long project are distinguishable on the fort wall. Mortar was as important as the bricks. General Totten himself wrote a treatise on mortar. Pulverized coral and sand collected from nearby keys and saltwater were mixed with natural cement imported from New England. Laborers, skilled masons, and carpenters had to be imported from the north. These workers were supplemented by slaves, mostly rented from owners in Key West. By 1857, there were almost 600 people working there seasonally, including 58 slaves. During the Civil War, military prisoners were put to work continuing the construction. (NPS.)

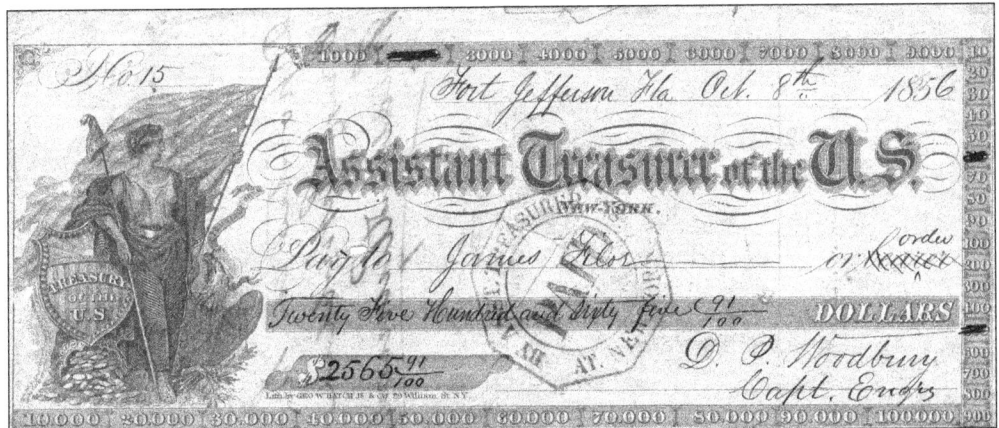

Army engineers were responsible for the expansion of slave holding in Key West. Locals accumulated slaves to rent out for fort construction. US senator Stephen Mallory, getting around an adverse conflict-of-interest judgement, had his wife rent them out. This image of a check from Woodbury to James Filor is for the 2019 equivalent of $77,000. Filor, also town marshal, inspired the local song that began, "Run, n---er, run! Filor will get you!" (MCPL.)

When the fort was being built, slave importation into the United States had been banned, and the US Navy patrolled to intercept slaver ships. The capture of the *Wildfire* (shown here) created a national drama. She was landed at Key West in 1860. A memorial is at Higg's Beach in Key West. Whether emancipation covered Federal-held Key West was not immediately clear, but after emancipation, former slaves declined to work at the forts. (MCPL.)

Woodbury and master mason George Phillips were responsible for one of the fort's most impressive features, its arches. The fort was designed with 2,000 repeated arches, double-arch vaulting, and thick pillars. The longevity and harmonious proportions of the arches were not by accident. Woodbury wrote a book entitled *Treatise on the Various Elements of Stability in the Well-Proportioned Arch*, published in 1858 during his tenure at the fort. The arch structure, and so the fort, held up amazingly well despite harsh conditions and storms. Over time, mortar dust rained down, and rainwater leaked around the ceiling bricks, in places producing stalactites, enhancing the fort's cave-like aspect. The monastery-like arches remain among the most memorable views within the fort. (Above, LOC; left, KH.)

The fort's design had its six sides joined by projecting tower-like bastions intended to provide withering crossfire. They contained gun rooms, powder magazines, and granite staircases that accessed the tiers. The walls were 8 feet thick and 50 feet tall from their base. Their foundations were sunk into the damp sand, causing subsidence of the heavy walls, a design flaw corrected in the 1850s. (NPS.)

A single doorway was meant to be the only entrance to the fort. It was framed in granite to hold two massive doors. This sally port had a second interior door so as to trap intruders who could be picked off from adjacent guardrooms. The gate was accessed by a drawbridge, installed in anticipation of the Civil War. In this 1901 photograph, the bridge had become more permanent. (NPS.)

The fort is surrounded by a moat, as shown in this 1965 image. Its seawall is a half mile in circumference. The moat is 70 feet wide. Its depth depended on the amount of sand, sediment, and solid waste that accumulated, requiring it occasionally to be dug out. Its construction was intermittent and not finished until 1873. Storms repeatedly battered and breached its retaining wall. (KH.)

The moat was also expected to be the fort's sewer. The effluent from privies drained into it. Sluice gates in the moat wall (lower left) were opened on the rising tide, allowing the moat to fill, and then closed until they were reopened at low tide to flush the moat's water. It did not work well. The condition of the moat plagued fort residents, leading to harsh criticism of the Army engineers. (NPS.)

The moat was also used as an aquarium and to hold sea turtles until butchering. Sharks have been its most infamous inhabitants in the public mind, a view encouraged by a 1936 film, *The Prisoner of Shark Island*. There was at least one real moat shark, put there during the Civil War as something of an experiment and entertainment. An image from the film is shown here (MCPL.)

The fort was designed to house 420 to 450 large guns. Cannon in the casemates were mounted on gun carriages able to pivot for aiming. A track on the casemate floor guided the gun carriage's wheels along an arc. The bastions housed smaller guns, 24-pound howitzers mounted on carriages. (NPS.)

Artillery came and went during the fort's history, being moved about the country to where the military needed it most. Many guns were never installed. Cannon and other munitions were subjected to weather, storms, and neglect. The gun inventory peaked at 243 during the Civil War. This image, from 1900, provides an idea of how the guns looked in the casemate. (NPS.)

Cannon on the top of the fort were to be mounted to shoot over the barbette. Also on the top level were traverse magazines designed as defensive barriers and ammunition storage. Through the years, the gun carriages deteriorated, and many cannon ended up on the ground; some fell when their carriages were burned to salvage their metal as scrap. This 1900 image shows guns mounted. (MCPL.)

The embrasures were to be reinforced with iron frames holding protective shutters, designed by Chief Totten himself, which were pushed open by cannon-fire gasses but were balanced to immediately rebound shut. Over the decades, the iron rusted, expanded, and destroyed the surrounding brickwork. After years of degradation, the National Park Service removed original iron shutter components and installed replicated components (shown here). This image shows the original design. (NPS.)

Over the long history of construction, most of the embrasures were not finished, leaving wide gaps in the walls. Exposure to weather over time widened some of these openings, eventually requiring their stabilization. These gaping unfinished holes in the fort's walls are among Fort Jefferson's more recognizable features. (NPS.)

Additional cannon were brought in the 1870s and 1880s. The largest were six 15-inch Rodman smoothbore cannon weighing 50,000 pounds and four Parrott rifled guns weighing 27,000 pounds. In 1873, a Rodman was mounted on an iron carriage on each bastion and the four Parrott guns were mounted on the front. In 1887, there were 72 unmounted guns at the fort. By 1913, only the 10 largest guns remained. (USGS.)

Unmounted cannon and the fort's supplies of cannonballs accumulated on the parade. In this image, soldiers are shown posing on the tubes. The shot was neatly stacked and decorative, a scene taken advantage of for photography. The armament laid about the fort for decades. Several times the fort's cannon, balls, cannon carriages, and other equipment were sold as scrap. (NPS.)

The fort walls enclosed the interior parade. An existing pond was filled and the ground elevated three feet with sand from Long Key and elsewhere. Soil was imported for a garden. The parade was used for housing soldiers and marching drills, thought essential to good soldiering. The interior was also intended for various buildings, most of which never got started or completed or were eventually removed due to their deteriorated condition. (MCPL.)

To accommodate the force size, the largest interior structure was the massive soldiers' barracks, shown in 1910, three stories tall and over 300 feet long, towering above the parapets. Never completed, it was under construction from 1862 to 1874. At times construction was a high priority, at other times not. It was intermittently used as storage, a hospital, and lodging. Soldiers mostly slept elsewhere. (MCPL.)

Part of the officers' quarters was among the first interior projects to be functional, probably because the engineering officers decided what was to be built first and these were their quarters. The occupied section to the right in the image was finished in 1850, while the rest of the 286-foot-long military officers' section continued under construction until the late 1870s but was never completed. (NPS.)

Living quarters for the engineering officers could be quite comfortable, unlike those occupied by soldiers, workers, and prisoners. This image shows a room and office with engineering equipment set out. Some officers and medical staff, as well as the lighthouse keepers, were accompanied by families and had separate housing. There was much shifting among quarters, especially as the Civil War increased personnel. (NPS.)

Associated with the engineers' quarters were stand-alone kitchen buildings positioned between the quarters and the fort. Nearby, privies for officers and families were finished by 1855, although the sewers were not all completed until 1865. This 1870 image shows the kitchens. The privies emptied to drains under the parade and then into the moat. The enlisted men's privies were outside the walls. (NPS.)

The parade was to have five ammunition magazines, but they were never finished. The largest magazine was under construction from 1862 to 1866. A smaller parade magazine was also partially built. The magazine's strongly built arch was meant to be covered with soil and be bombproof. The magazine was designed to moderate its interior climate, as maintaining gunpowder in the dampness of the Dry Tortugas was a continuing challenge. (KH.)

A hotshot furnace used for heating cannonballs was completed in 1863. Cannonballs were heated up, retrieved at the bottom of the shoot, filed, and carried with tongs to the cannoneers. This is thought to be the largest and last such furnace constructed in the United States. As shown in this 1970 image, its structure degraded over time. (KH.)

The parade also contained the pre-existing lighthouse and keeper's quarters. Various accommodations inside and outside the fort were developed for medical purposes, including parts of the barracks, casemates, and buildings outside the walls, depending on the current need. During epidemics, hospitals were built on other islands. (UM.)

Annually only 30 inches of rain fall on the Dry Tortugas, so 100 cisterns were designed to hold up to 1.5 million gallons of rainfall. Many became salty although used for washing and cooking. A 92,000-gallon cistern under the parade was successful and is still in use. The cistern roof (shown) was meant to be the floor of a never-built chapel. A condenser unit produced water during the Civil War. (NPS.)

The logistical difficulty of getting sufficient building materials for such a massive edifice located in the ocean and serviced by sailing vessels can scarcely be appreciated today. Wreckage of one supply vessel remains accessible. The Brick Wreck carried bricks dated to 1857–1861, indicating it sank about the time of the Civil War. These bricks, like many other loads of supplies and materiel, never made it to the fort. (NPS.)

Although it is a foolish man who builds his house on sand, the fort was. By 1859, parts of the wall had settled 12 inches, visible today by visually tracing the mortar joints against the moat's horizontal water surface, as shown in this 1964 image. In 1865, engineers decided to temporarily stop work on the fort's second-tier iron embrasures and associated stonework. (NPS.)

Coincident with building the fort, the engineers undertook to build another lighthouse closer to the reef on Loggerhead Key. The light, refined by the fort's engineer Woodbury, was completed in 1858. The light station (shown here) also had a keeper's house, cookhouse, fuel storage, and cisterns. Initially, the Loggerhead Key tower was left this yellow-red brick color. (UM.)

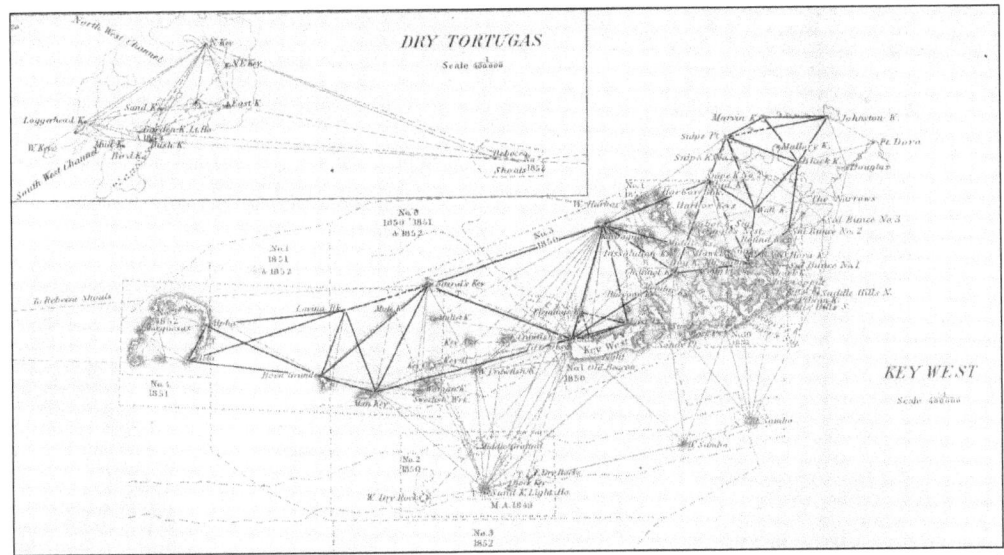

The federal government also undertook to conduct a definitive survey of the Florida coast, reef, and keys. Alexander Bache and F.H. Gerdes of the US Coast Survey were responsible for the work. This 1857 image shows results from 1845 to 1857. The coast surveys were done with the highest of contemporary accuracy. (NYPL.)

Rebecca Channel, 20 miles east of Garden Key, was a crucial 60-foot-deep north-south passage. Lt. George Meade installed an iron screw-pile lighthouse, but it washed away in 1854. In 1879, a 75-foot-tall beacon was erected, and in 1886, a replacement screw-pile lighthouse was installed (shown). It did not go well for the isolated lighthouse keepers there; two died, with one committing suicide by jumping into the ocean. (USNA.)

Coordinated with the coast survey, Alexander Bache invited Harvard naturalist Louis Agassiz (shown) to conduct a biological survey of the Florida reefs. In 1855, Professor Agassiz arrived at the Tortugas with Chief Totten himself. Bache, Agassiz, and Totten were among America's most famous and distinguished scientists. Earlier in his career, Totten had been a surveyor for Bache; there is no doubt he was quite interested to see his great fort. (NYPL.)

Agassiz's overriding task was to assess natural history aspects of the reef's danger to shipping. He sampled widely and made extensive collections and observations on the structure and biota of the reef. One of his most important findings was calculating coral growth rate on a brick in Fort Jefferson's moat. Agassiz's influence was to play a continuing role in future biological and geological studies at the Tortugas. (NOAA.)

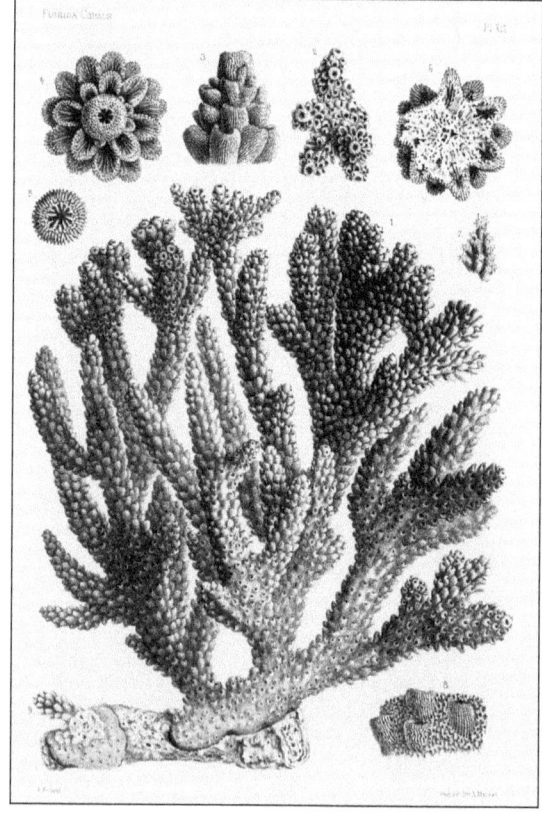

Three

THE CIVIL WAR

At the Civil War's start, the half-finished fort was ill prepared to defend itself. In 1860, the fort's codesigner Capt. Montgomery Meigs was appointed engineer in charge and traveled the South to meet with the fort's suppliers. He reported with alarm about the Southern mood should Abraham Lincoln win the election. At Fort Jefferson, Meigs found only the lighthouse keeper and family, 50 workers, few arms, and no cannon. He ordered over 200 wall breaches closed, eliminated construction bridges, and installed a drawbridge. The fort's command passed to the Regular Army when Maj. L.G. Arnold arrived on January 18, 1861. One day after arriving, it is told, although undocumented contemporaneously, that he bluffed off a Confederate-sympathizing privateer. Both Fort Jefferson and Fort Taylor in Key West were secured by Federal soldiers for the duration of the war. Key West's diverse citizenry was of divided loyalties. Former Key West resident Stephen Mallory became secretary of the Confederate navy; others were Unionists. During the war, Fort Jefferson was a port of call for ships blockading the coast. Islands adjacent to the harbor were ordered fortified. Although the fort never saw conflict, the potential was there from both Florida rebels and European powers in the Caribbean. Late in 1861, the fort also became a military prison. Convicted Union soldiers were sentenced to hard labor building the fort, which housed as many as 800 prisoners and a succession of military garrisons. Hundreds of people lived in the fort, including soldiers, prisoners, engineers, surgeons, and civilian families.

As the Civil War was ending, added to the prisoners were four known as "the Conspirators," who had been convicted in military court of participation in the assassination of Pres. Abraham Lincoln. Edman "Ned" Spangler, Samuel Arnold, Michael O'Laughlen, and Samuel Mudd arrived just three months after the assassination. These, particularly Dr. Mudd, became famous, as did their prison, owing to their much-publicized complaints. Yellow fever broke out in 1867, and Mudd helped treat victims. Surviving Conspirators were pardoned by Pres. Andrew Johnson as his term ended in 1869. As other prisoners were pardoned, the prison population and troop strength decreased.

With war looming, Union-leaning members of the Lighthouse Board conducted inspection tours, ostensibly of lighthouses but actually to determine the situation at coastal fortifications. Board member William Farrar "Baldy" Smith (shown) inspected Fort Jefferson. He encouraged it be defended against the State of Florida, which was demanding the surrender of federal properties. Smith, long-term engineering secretary of the Lighthouse Board, later became president of the International Telegraph Company. (LOC.)

Initially, it was up to the Army engineers to secure Fort Jefferson. Captain Meigs (shown) was the fort's well-respected designer who, at that moment, happened to have been exiled back to the fort for refusing to go along with corruption of his departmental leadership. Meigs went on to become Union quartermaster general. It was he who turned Robert E. Lee's family estate into a Union graveyard, Arlington National Cemetery. (LOC.)

The new fort commander, Major Arnold, knew Florida well from his experience in the Seminole Wars. Upon his arrival, he reported the poor state of defense but complimented Captain Meigs's work. He immediately sent Meigs to Fort Taylor, where he secured munitions including 10 guns, which they set to work mounting. Arnold obtained men and ordnance and organized defenses. Within weeks, the fort was reported ready. (USNA.)

Another personage central to Fort Jefferson's Civil War story was, perhaps surprisingly, physician-scientist Joseph Bassett Holder (shown). He, his wife, and son wrote much of what is known about civilian life at the fort. Holder, an accomplished naturalist, was recommended for a dual job of engineers' physician and resident naturalist by Louis Agassiz and the Smithsonian's Spenser Baird. The hiring decision was certainly that of Chief Totten, himself also a Smithsonian regent. (LOC.)

Holding Fort Jefferson was a strategic and public relations coup. This 1861 *Harper's Weekly* illustration gives an impression of the fort at the start of the war. A strong and apparently completed fort is shown bustling with activity. Near the over-tall lighthouse, a large American flag flies from a disproportionately tall flagpole, showing symbolically that Fort Jefferson, at the deepest point within the secessionist South, remained securely in Union hands. (MCPL.)

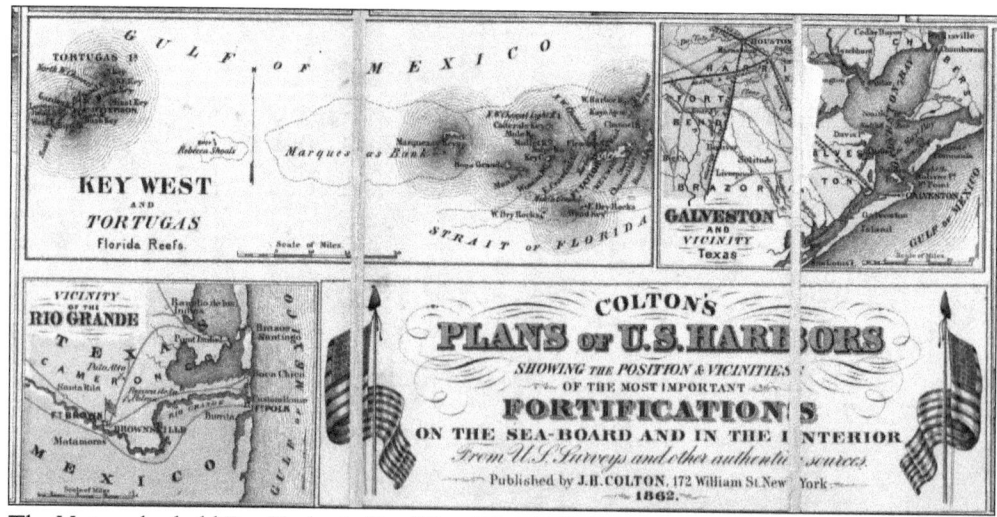

The Union also held Fort Taylor in Key West. This 1862 illustration shows the two South Florida Union forts. Holding these and Pensacola was key in the Union's blockading Confederate supply lines. They also provided a deterrent against European nations that might have sided with the Confederacy from their Caribbean colonies. Key West became headquarters for the East Gulf Blockading Squadron, which captured over 300 ships. (LOC.)

Soon additional soldiers began to arrive at the fort. By September 1861, Fort Jefferson had 500 men in arms and, by 1862, over 1,000. Units periodically were posted to the fort and then reassigned. Units included New Hampshire and New York volunteer infantry and Pennsylvania infantry. The volunteer New York Zouaves, illustrated prior to their posting, were forced into Regular Army uniforms and became a troublemaking lot. (SLAF.)

Some soldiers documented their military life in diaries and letters home, including Calvin Shedd, who arrived in 1862 with the 7th New Hampshire Volunteer Infantry, and Harrison Herrick, who arrived in 1864 with the 110th New York Volunteers. They wrote of marching drills, equipment upkeep, boredom, bad food, mosquitoes, heat, humidity, sickness, superior officers, and deaths of comrades. Soldiers did not like Fort Jefferson. Repostings elsewhere were well received. (NPS.)

During the war, Army and engineer officers occupied the partially finished officer quarters. With the soldiers' barracks incomplete, most were housed in damp, dark, boarded-over second-tier gun rooms (shown), temporary buildings, and tents. Soldiers practiced with artillery, guarded, and drilled. The Northern army knew nothing about the tropics. Soldiers complained about junior officers who called for extended drills in full woolen uniforms in the midday sun. (LOC.)

Toward the end of the war, freedmen were recruited to join the Union army. The 10th Corps d'Afrique Infantry was organized in Louisiana in 1862 to serve along the Gulf Coast. In 1866, its successor, the 82nd US Colored Troops, was, for a short time, posted to the fort. Their arrival was not welcomed by Southern-sympathizing prisoners, nor by many of the all-white Army troops. (LOC.)

Fort Jefferson's role as a military prison began in 1861, when 53 soldiers charged with mutiny arrived. Prisoners were primarily Union soldiers court-marshaled for offenses such as desertion, cowardice, mutiny, insubordination, or theft, not always fairly. Later, Confederate and civilian prisoners arrived. As of February 1864, when Lincoln changed the penalty for desertion from death to "imprisonment on the Dry Tortugas," the prison population at Fort Jefferson climbed. (NPS.)

During the Civil War, the fort continued in command of the Regular Army. The soldiers manned the fort, prepared for its defense, and guarded the prisoners. The engineers continued their charge to build the fort and were responsible for work of the prisoners. As the war progressed, the fort's defense became less of a concern as the potential of a Confederate or foreign challenge diminished. (UM.)

The fort, with hundreds of military, civilian, and prisoner residents, became a town. There were a lot of people crowded into a small, unfinished, quite isolated space and temporary accommodations and buildings. This image shows the parade with trees, mostly unfinished buildings, and stored supplies and armaments. (UM.)

Extensive facilities were also located outside the fort's walls on the remaining few acres of Garden Key. Temporary buildings housed storage, workshops, the engineers' hospital, Holder's research lab, and water condenser buildings. This image gives an impression of the crowded facilities located outside the walls. (UM.)

Provisioning the fort for so many residents was a constant challenge. War and sea conditions interfered with supply boats. Private merchants, called sutlers, ran commissaries. James Watts Robinson, Fort Jefferson's Civil War sutler, brought supplies from Key West to sell to prisoners, civilians, and soldiers, providing credit for purchases between paydays. A wooden cabin was built as his shop. This is an image of a typical Civil War–era sutler's store. (UM.)

Dampness meant stored food became infested with mold and weevils. Even hardtack became inedible. Stories abounded of worms and insects infesting the food. Government provisions were supplemented by gardening, fishing, turtles, coconuts, and eggs. Livestock was kept on the out-islands, Bush Key being called Hog Island. Soldiers received permission to leave the fort to fish or collect turtles or eggs. This is an illustration of shark fishing. (KH.)

All three of the Holders eventually wrote about life at the fort during the Civil War, Joseph and Emily in articles and son Charles in a thinly fictionalized novel. The Holders were assigned one of the houses (shown at left). Other families included those of the lighthouse keeper, other doctors, and officers. The image below is a portrait of officers and their wives at the fort. The families would hold dances, picnics, and other such events. One story is of them going over to Loggerhead Key for a party and to turn turtles at night. They would periodically sail to Key West for personal reprovisioning and relief from the crowded fort. (Both, UM.)

As a physician, Holder reported to the chief of engineers, but he was also a scientist reporting to the Smithsonian. His laboratory was perched over the moat, and he explored the keys and reefs widely, making and recording observations, many of which he later published. This image is of a page from one of his articles. After departing in 1866, Holder became a well-known biologist, museum curator, and textbook author. (KH.)

To conduct his biological surveys of the reef, shallows, and islands, Joseph Holder had access to boats and volunteer prisoners. One prisoner-helper, called "Fat Charlie," seemed to end up in all sorts of mischief. Holder would observe and gather specimens, including large fish such as sharks, which he once put in the moat. This image shows Holder and his party in boats beached on an island near the fort. (UM.)

Dr. Holder started a minstrel show called the Key Lime Theater, performed by prisoners (shown). Theater admission fees bought limes used to combat scurvy caused by limited access to fruits and vegetables other than trickles from Havana or Key West. In 1865, Holder discovered that the native dune plant sea purslane was efficacious and had it served. He wrote it was well-liked; others reported it was awful. (KH.)

Other health problems persisted. Casemate cells were damp and infested with rats, bedbugs, mosquitoes, and mold. Sanitation was an unsolvable problem. Using the moat for flushing waste was a disaster, and it became unbearably filthy. Smells permeated the fort, causing distress, as medical theory held that diseases such as cholera was caused by miasmas, poisonous or night vapors from decaying matter. It was, apparently, appalling. (SLAF.)

Illness prevailed among soldiers and prisoners, who were often too sick to work. Fort Jefferson was not without adequate medical staffing. In addition to Dr. Holder, who was responsible for the engineers and their prisoner workers, a succession of doctors served the soldiers. Deaths were commonplace. Those who died were buried on outlying islands, as shown in this 1864 drawing of the Army hospital and cemetery on Sand Key. (MCPL.)

Over 2,200 prisoners passed through during the fort's 10 years as a prison, averaging a population of about 500. Their hard labor was meant to make up for the lack of civilian workers in building the fort. Many had valuable civilian skills that were well utilized. Treated like normal workers during the day, at night, prisoners were locked into boarded-over casemates (shown here). (NPS.)

Soldier-prisoners were subjected to military discipline that, despite stories to the contrary, was not exceptional for a military prison at the time. Prisoner punishments for bad behavior included extra duty, carrying a cannonball, solitary confinement, having thumbs tied to a scaffold, hauling sand, or being dunked in the ocean. This cartoon from one of Holder's articles shows shackled prisoners managing a ball and chain. (KH.)

Escapes and attempted escapes did occur. Prisoners hid aboard departing ships, stole boats, or swam to Loggerhead Key, one by floating his ball and chain, shown in this cartoon. Some were successful, or at least never heard from again. Owing to publicity generated by some of the prisoners, the Tortugas gained fame as a notorious prison. Prisoners regularly arrived and also departed after pardons or review of often irregular courts-martial. (KH.)

The four "Conspirators," also called "state prisoners" to distinguish them from military prisoners, arrived secretly on the USS *Florida* on July 14, 1865. With their arrival, the Dry Tortugas came to public prominence. John Wilkes Booth had been killed, other Conspirators hanged, and these four imprisoned. Public interest bordered on hysteria. Dr. Samuel Mudd is represented on the right in this cartoon, without a noose around his neck. (LOC.)

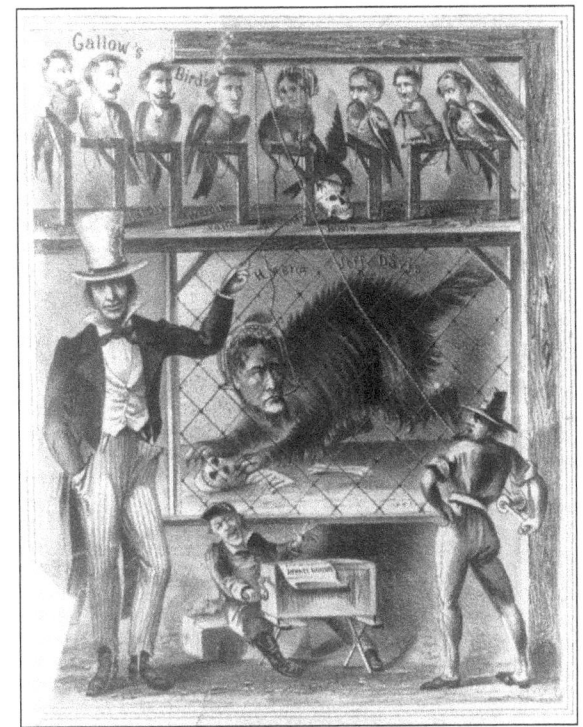

Samuel Mudd (shown) was a country doctor, tobacco farmer, and slave owner who set John Wilkes Booth's leg and sheltered him overnight. Ned Spangler worked at Ford's Theater. Samuel Arnold was a serial anti-Lincoln plotter and Booth friend. Michael O'Laughlen was also a previous plotter. In October, they were joined by Confederate operative George St. Leger Grenfell. These five were famous nationwide, and Grenfell's case drew international attention. (NLM.)

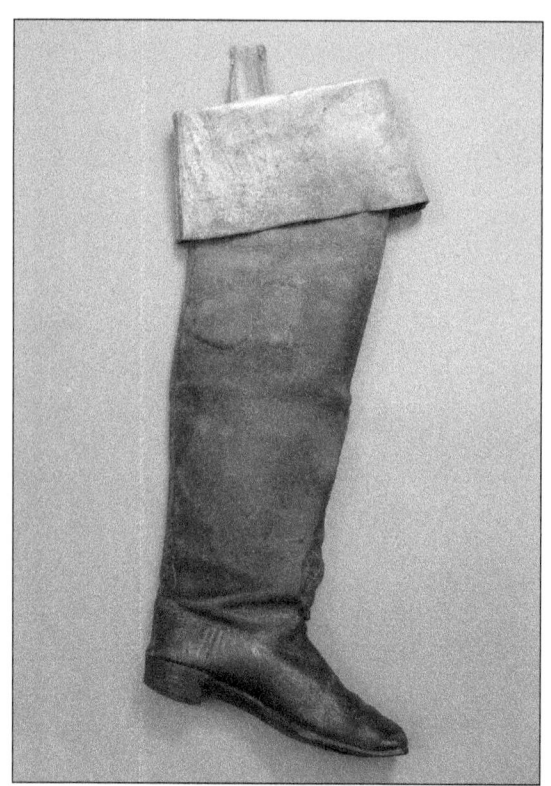

Dr. Mudd, the main celebrity prisoner, was a strong Southern sympathizer involved in a previous plot to kidnap Lincoln. Booth's boot (shown) was in his possession. Mudd delayed notifying authorities, lied about his story, and stated that he had not recognized Booth despite Booth's fake theater beard having slipped down, revealing his face. Mudd and Booth had had previous face-to-face business dealings. Mudd always insisted he was innocent. (LOC.)

Dr. Mudd did not endear himself to his jailers when he tried to escape only two months after his arrival. The absence of the infamous prisoner was easily noticed, and he was soon found, though not cleverly ensconced in a cannon as depicted for *Harper's Magazine*. He hid on an unarmed transport vessel by stuffing himself under floorboards in the hold, from which he emerged to avoid a searching bayonet. (KH.)

Samuel Mudd's prison life was not improved by his highly publicized escape attempt. New rules were imposed. Mudd was shackled, guarded, confined to the fort, and sent to what was popularly called the "dungeon," which it was not, as the fort had no basement. The dungeons actually were secure storage rooms and casemate cells. The actual location of his solitary confinement is unrecorded, but a cell soon was popularly ascribed to being his dungeon and was once labeled with the words, "Who so entereth here leaveth all hope behind," from Canto III of Dante's *Inferno*. For nearly all of his stay, Mudd's room actually was right above the sally port, having thin escape-proof loopholes. Park visitors can take a look at both the room traditionally said to be his dungeon and the Conspirator's sally port casemate cell. (Both, NPS.)

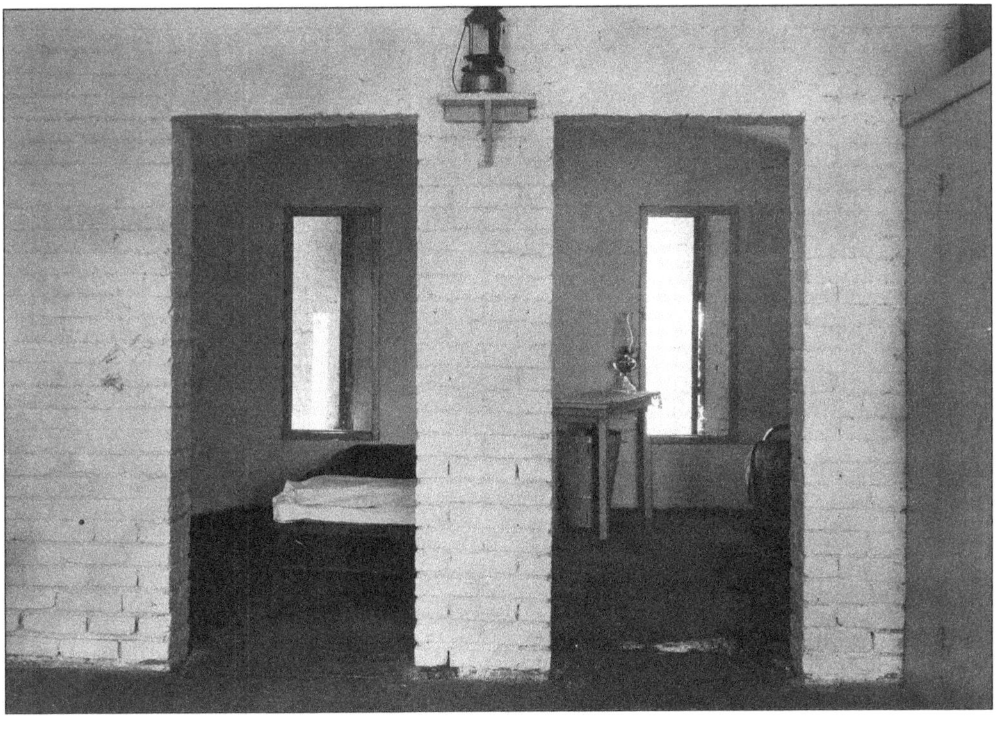

Dr. Mudd was not a happy man at the fort. Emily Holder described him as restless and brooding. Dr. Holder dismissed him from his hospital for misadministering medication. Mudd's letters expressed how badly he felt treated. One complaint was the leaky roof. The Conspirators etched a still-visible shallow trench into the cell floor to drain rain. Once out of irons, Mudd had daytime freedom within the fort as he went about his work shift, sweeping the bastion stairs, gardening, and carpentry. His garden tending met little success, despite his being a farmer. He showed considerable talent in the carpenter's shop, as evidenced by the inlaid table that he made (below). His portrait (left) was taken in the woodshop. Mudd also spent his time writing petitions and letters, which provide detailed documentation of his time imprisoned at Fort Jefferson. (Both, NPS.)

Samuel Arnold was the greatest publicist for complaining about conditions. "Day after day," he wrote, "the miserable existence was being dragged out, intermixed with sickness, bodily suffering, want, and pinching hunger." Previous to the Ford's Theater plot, Arnold had twice conspired to kidnap President Lincoln. After release, he returned to Baltimore. He revisited the fort in 1898 and, in 1902, published his story in newspaper articles. (LOC.)

Michael O'Laughlen was a childhood friend of John Wilkes Booth, with whom he had conspired to kidnap President Lincoln so as to create a prisoner exchange. He had been informed about Booth's plan for capturing Lincoln at Ford's Theater and came to Washington, DC, at the time of the assassination. He died of yellow fever at Fort Jefferson in 1876. (LOC.)

Edman Spangler was likely the least culpable of the Conspirators and, in fact, had been acquitted on the conspiracy charge. As a carpenter and stagehand at Ford's Theater, he knew and admired the famous actor Booth. Found guilty of helping Booth escape, he always professed innocence. After prison, he went back to work for John T. Ford, of Ford's Theater, and later lived on Samuel Mudd's farm. (LOC.)

Englishman George St. Leger Grenfell was a soldier of fortune and Southern spy. Condemned to be hanged, his sentence was commuted at the demand of the British Parliament. Grenfell was an idiosyncratic character who theatrically resisted prison authority. In 1868, when an officer whom Grenfell had set up for court-marshal returned to the fort, Grenfell stole a small boat, rowed into a storm, and was never seen again. (KH.)

During the summer, or "sick months," yellow fever and break-bone fever (dengue fever) were intermittently epidemic in Havana and Key West, but tightly controlled Fort Jefferson escaped epidemics until 1867. This over-the-top drawing suggests how serious the situation was viewed to be. It would be 40 years before it was shown that mosquitoes, which breed in standing water in such places as the fort's uncovered cisterns, spread the disease. (LOC.)

The yellow fever episode of 1867 provided Samuel Mudd's public redemption. When the fort physician died, Mudd, assisted by Grenfell, took over until a replacement arrived a day later, after which he continued to assist until getting sick himself and being cared for by Edman Spangler. Of 270 cases, there were 38 deaths. Mudd and contemporary doctors treated victims by purging and heat. The incurable disease required palliative care. (NPS.)

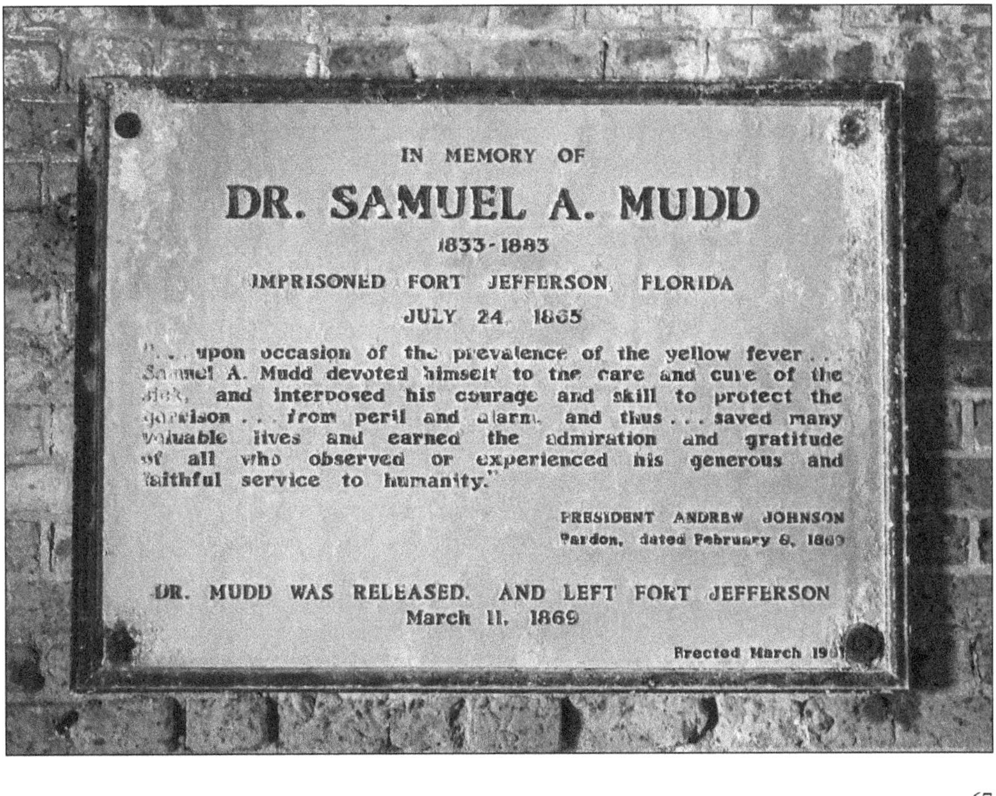

IN MEMORY OF
DR. SAMUEL A. MUDD
1833-1883

IMPRISONED FORT JEFFERSON FLORIDA

JULY 24, 1865

"... upon occasion of the prevalence of the yellow fever... Samuel A. Mudd devoted himself to the care and cure of the sick, and interposed his courage and skill to protect the garrison... from peril and alarm, and thus... saved many valuable lives and earned the admiration and gratitude of all who observed or experienced his generous and faithful service to humanity."

PRESIDENT ANDREW JOHNSON
Pardon, dated February 8, 1869

DR. MUDD WAS RELEASED, AND LEFT FORT JEFFERSON
March 11, 1869

Erected March 19__

Samuel's wife, Sarah (shown), repeatedly wrote pleas and personally visited President Johnson. Her argument for clemency became Mudd's service in the epidemic. Johnson handed the clemency paper directly to Sarah just prior to General Grant taking over as president, whom it was assumed would be less amenable. Mudd was released on February 8, 1869. In fact, all surviving Conspirators were pardoned after serving only four years of their sentences. (NPS.)

Dr. Richard D. Mudd (shown) led a multi-decade campaign to clear his grandfather's name. In 1959, he persuaded Congress to authorize the previously pictured plaque recognizing Mudd's medical services. The plaque, which can be seen in the fort today, is silent on his guilt or innocence. In 2015, about 80 Mudd descendants toured the fort on the 150th anniversary of Samuel's incarceration and of Lincoln's assassination. (HM.)

Four

AN AMERICAN BACKWATER

Although after the Civil War, the federal government initially continued building and rearming the fort, this was short-lived. Rifled shot was deemed to make such forts obsolete, and in 1883, the fort officially was declared to be defenseless against ironclad ships. With Army-manned coastal forts considered ineffective, the mobile Navy took over coastal defenses. In 1886, following a renewed yellow fever outbreak and hurricanes, the Army removed its garrison, leaving behind only a few caretakers, and in 1889, it pulled out completely, ending its 40 years of responsibility for Fort Jefferson. Lighthouses, however, continued to be a priority, and the Tortugas lights were upgraded and continued to be manned.

    The Dry Tortugas took on a succession of replacement responsibilities. The Marine Hospital Service set up an outpost of the Key West Quarantine Station, and the Navy established a coal refueling station. The Dry Tortugas became a location for winter maneuvers of the Atlantic Fleet. Having taken on coal, it was from Fort Jefferson that the USS *Maine* departed for her destiny. The Spanish-American War, in 1898, saw Fort Jefferson briefly rearmed and regarrisoned by the 5th US Infantry. But after that short war, the fort's utility resumed its decline. In 1900, the quarantine station closed, and the Navy's responsibility was transferred to the Key West Naval Station. Hurricanes and increased use of oil as fuel encouraged the Navy to abandon its Tortugas coal depot in 1908. In 1912, following a fire that burned down the lighthouse's residence, the keeper and family left. For a brief interlude, the Dry Tortugas were activated for World War I as a coastal observation station, seaplane base, and wireless station.

    As changes in military strategy made the unfinished fort irrelevant, its future prospects dimmed. Even when the hospital service and Navy had facilities there, their interests did not extend beyond what was necessary for their mission. The tropical climate, hurricanes, fires, souvenir hunting, vandalism, and gravity expedited the increasingly ghostly edifice's decline.

Although prisoners departed after the Civil War, construction continued on the fort (shown). Craftsmen and laborers, mostly new immigrants, were again imported from the north, leaving during the hot, damp, stormy sick season. By 1870, the officers' quarters and soldier barracks were well along. Starting in 1872, the fort was modernized with new guns and strengthened magazines. (MCPL.)

During the second yellow fever epidemic in 1873, the Tortugas made minor medical history. Among attending assistant surgeons were Harvey E. Brown Jr. and Joseph Yates Porter (shown). Brown, later senior surgeon of the Army, was the foremost authority on quarantine and published on his yellow fever experience at the fort. Key West native Porter later established Florida's public health service and its strict, and not unbiased, quarantine policies. (MCPL.)

After the Civil War, Key West, shown in 1880, continued to prosper. In 1878, Mallory Line steamships began connecting Key West directly to New York. Commands stationed in Key West managed the region's military matters. By 1890, Key West was not only the largest town in Florida but among the nation's wealthiest. The Tortugas were a way station for ships coming to or from Key West Harbor and naval base. (MCPL.)

Following the 1878 end of the unsuccessful Ten Years' War, Key West's economy was buoyed by an influx of Cuban refugees providing workers for the cigar industry (shown). By 1890, Key West's almost 130 factories produced over 100 million cigars, and Cubans were the cultural majority in Key West. The Key West economy was also driven by exploitation of natural resources, especially sponges and sea turtles. (MCPL.)

The sponge fishery took off after 1849, when a market was found in New York. It expanded after the Civil War and, by 1890, employed more than 1,300 men and 350 hook boats working the shallow banks. Others supported processing, auction, and shipping of sponges. This image shows sponge trimmers at work. Other memorabilia can be seen at the Key West Sponge Market. (MCPL.)

Catch boats plied the shallow waters, including the Tortugas Bank, to net sea turtles. Expanding in the late 1800s, the harvest fueled production of Key West's international delicacy, turtle soup. Tens of thousands of green turtles were killed until the population crashed. This 1898 image shows turtles at the kraals, now the site of the Key West Turtle Museum. (MCPL.)

Following hurricane damage in 1873 and 1875, the War Department decided to replace the then-50-year old lighthouse on Garden Key. The new light tower, 37 feet high set atop a 55-foot-tall bastion, was first lit in 1876. The Dry Tortugas' third lighthouse, the second on Garden Key, was a hexagonal, three-story tower made of boilerplate iron. The iron tower was lighter than brick and less stressed the walls. (NPS.)

The keeper's quarters continued to occupy the parade (shown). The old light's lens was transferred to the new, and the Tortugas' first lighthouse was torn down in 1877. Its foundation floor remains on the parade. The new lighthouse on Garden Key, now an iconic feature of the fort, was featured on a US postage stamp in 2009. (NPS.)

Out on Loggerhead Key, the lighthouse withstood the 1875 hurricane, unexpectedly given the temporary repairs made after the 1871 hurricane. So plans to replace it were scrapped, and improvements were made instead. A boathouse was built in 1880, and extensive repairs and renovations were undertaken in 1899. In 1909, a new lens changed its fixed characteristic to flashing, and incandescent oil vapor replaced kerosene as fuel. (SLAF.)

In 1888, Garden, Loggerhead, and Bird Keys were made part of the system of national quarantine stations. Tent housing for detainees, dockage, and disinfecting and fumigation facilities were created. This image shows public health officials at the fort. Although the military reclaimed command of the fort in 1893, the quarantine facility continued until 1900, receiving returnees from the Spanish-American War. (NPS.)

The Revenue Service and Navy called at Fort Jefferson in support of their operations, including anti-smuggling campaigns. Smuggling took on additional political seriousness as gun runners called filibusters, including a future Florida governor, carried arms to Cuban revolutionaries. This image shows a revenue cutter docked at Fort Jefferson in 1897. (NPS.)

Both military ships and civilian yachts in transit to the United States had to report to a quarantine station. They disembarked at the fort during their ship's decontamination process to be checked by the public health doctors. This couple is shown walking along the moat in 1899. (NPS.)

The refueling station on Garden Key was built during the 1890s to service the Navy's fleet of steamships. Docks and other facilities were built outside the fort on the beachfront of Garden Key. The image above shows visitors inspecting construction of the south coal shed. Navy ships moored to the coaling docks, where they were loaded with coal and with water made in a distillation plant. The image below shows ongoing construction at the south dock with the coal storage shed in the background. In 1897, the largest fleet of US Navy ships since the Civil War assembled at Key West for maneuvers near the Dry Tortugas. In 1898, a total of 23 US Navy ships called at the Tortugas harbor. (Above, NPS; below, SLAF.)

Ordered from Key West to New Orleans, the USS Maine stopped at the Dry Tortugas to take on coal. Once there in January 1898, she was redirected to Cuba. The stated mission was goodwill, to show the flag, and to protect American interests during an ongoing Cuban revolt against Spain. Spanish authorities received her cordially, but she blew up in Havana Harbor, killing 266 crew members. A mine was blamed. Newspaper coverage used the incident to help incite the Spanish-American War, starting in April 1898. A later study showed the explosion more likely came from within the ship, from a fire originating in her coal stores—coal taken on in the Tortugas. The Maine, in fact, suffered from design flaws in the separation of coal and ammunition storage. A memorial to the USS Maine may be seen in the Key West Cemetery. (LOC.)

With the outbreak of war 100 miles away in Cuba, the Army returned to Fort Jefferson. With enlisted men's accommodations uninhabitable, the soldiers created a camp on the parade ground, shown in these 1898 images. Although soldiers were deployed to the fort, the war lasted only until December 1898, and the fort saw no action. With the short Spanish-American War effort being headquartered in Tampa, Fort Jefferson's role was primarily as a refueling and quarantine stop for ship transports. A submarine cable was laid connecting the Tortugas with Key West. (Both, NPS.)

Along with the soldiers came new cannon, including the addition of Rodman guns and Parrott rifles. Rodmans were famous for their strong tube. The rifled cannon were famous for accuracy, so long as they did not blow up. This photograph, from 1900, shows the cannon and also the lighthouse keeper's quarters and barracks in the background. (SLAF.)

Until 1900, the isolated fort continued to function as a quarantine station for naval ships returning from Cuba or otherwise inbound to the United States. During the Spanish-American War, 400 soldiers died in battle in Cuba, but 2,000 died from yellow fever. The postwar American occupation force passed through quarantine before coming back to the country. This is a photograph of quarantined arrivals awaiting clearance. (NPS.)

With the conflict's end, the Army again departed, but the Navy continued to enhance its coaling station, dredging the channels to 30 feet to accommodate its ships. Marines replaced the Army in manning the fort, renaming the soldiers' barracks the Marine barracks. The station was operational by 1901. This image shows a ship at the dock in 1902 with the coal storage sheds in the background. (SLAF.)

The coaling station's distillation plant could make 60,000 gallons of fresh water a day. The water was stored on-site until loaded on ships. To the left and center of this 1902 image are the storage tanks and cisterns. The plant's smokestack is to the right. When it was decommissioned, the condensation plant was shipped to the Navy's new base at Guantanamo Bay, Cuba. (NPS.)

Hurricanes in 1904 and 1910 severely impacted the coaling facility, as well as the officers' quarters and Marine barracks. This is an image of the wrecked conveyors in 1910. The Navy chose to abandon the Tortugas station while continuing to operate its coaling station in Key West as it transitioned from coal to oil-powered ships. The Navy's presence in the Caribbean and Gulf refocused on its Guantanamo base. (USGS.)

The government presence in the Dry Tortugas fell to the US Lighthouse Service, whose job was the lights, not the fort. The fort's condition continued to degrade. Brickwork was weakened by erosion of the sand-and-saltwater-based mortar. The 1912 fire burned and collapsed roofs and the keeper's house, leading to the harbor light's automation. This image suggests the progress of degradation of the quarters and kitchen buildings. (NPS.)

The lack of on-site security allowed visitors to do what they pleased. Even the lighthouse was defaced. This image shows the thoroughly graffitied main gate. Other markings decorate the lintels of the windows that once were part of the historic cell occupied by Dr. Mudd and the other Lincoln Conspirators. The moat bridge has lost part of its deck. (NPS.)

The now-abandoned fort was scavenged. In this image, salvors who had contracted for the fort's metal are shown lowering a cannon down to the ground to be carried away for recycling. Despite being auctioned off in 1913, the 10 large cannon remained on the top of the terreplein, probably because they were not worth the cost to move. (NPS.)

As Fort Jefferson was abandoned during the first decade of the 1900s, the town of Key West boomed. In 1912, its centuries-long isolation ended as the railroad was completed to the town. This image is of the inaugural train in 1912. The region, including the Tortugas, was opened to new residents and visitors. Goods from Cuba or the soon-to-be opened Panama Canal could now be transshipped in Key West. (MCPL.)

At the station in Key West, the train met passenger ships of the Peninsular & Occidental Steam Ship Company (shown), which could take passengers directly to Cuba. Adventurous Key West visitors could stay in town and charter boats to go explore Fort Jefferson or fish the Dry Tortugas reefs. (MCPL.)

Key West, well-populated, prosperous, and now a tourist destination, provided a steady stream of visitors to the fort. Visitors boated over and explored the fort and its surroundings, often taking souvenir shells, bricks, and coral back with them. The image above is from 1910 showing a rather official party dining with the Navy within the fort. The image below, also from 1910, shows a party visiting Loggerhead Key. (Both, MCPL.)

In the late 1800s, sea bathing became exceptionally popular. It had come to be considered healthy, and seaside resorts emerged to provide sea bathing opportunities. On the Dry Tortugas, people could hardly help but take advantage of its beaches and waters. This 1898 image shows men in full bathing costumes at the beach. (NPS.)

Seeing the mysterious, crumbling, enormous fort was a goal of most visitors. It was open to being explored and full of interesting artifacts and stories, with some of them true. The remaining cannonball stacks in the parade often were put to good photographic use, as shown in this image. (NPS.)

Starting in 1919, a new activity opened up in the Tortugas: bootlegging. Although the Tortugas were not a smuggling destination, for the 13 years of Prohibition until 1933, they were a waypoint for movement of smuggled spirits from Havana and Matanzas to a welcoming Key West, which never really accepted the concept of prohibition. (USCG.)

Some of the visitors to the fort apparently had a similar opinion. This image, from the first decade of the 1900s, shows a costumed party of 19 posing on the parade. Among the variety of meaningful costumes is a man dressed as Carrie Nation, hatchet in hand. The reasons for the well-executed costumes are not known—perhaps it was an early expression of what became Key West's Fantasy Fest 60 years later. (NPS.)

Five

Birds and Reefs

About the time the military utility of Fort Jefferson was definitively waning, except for its very minor supportive roles in the Spanish-American War and World War I, the Dry Tortugas' biological values came to be better appreciated. Naturalist W.E.D. Scott visited the quarantine station on Garden Key in 1890, becoming the first to document the Tortugas' impressive spring bird migration. In 1904, Herbert K. Job, a minister who became devoted to birds and bird conservation, visited the tern colony as he was retracing Audubon's path through South Florida for his book *Wild Wings*, which proved influential with the national bird conservation movement. It also influenced Theodore Roosevelt, who in 1908 declared the Tortugas a bird reserve, giving responsibility to the Department of Agriculture. Roosevelt's bird reservations were intended to protect seabird colonies along the American coasts from the massive harvest of feathers for use in fashion. The bird colonies on the Dry Tortugas had their own centuries-long history of exploitation. The terns were killed and their eggs collected for food, as was reported over 70 years previously by John James Audubon, who had made note of the huge take by eggers from Havana. Egging persisted as a source of food through the Civil War and beyond by collectors from Key West. By the end of decades of exploitation, there were only a few thousand seabirds left.

Starting in 1903 and continuing for over 30 years, the Tortugas Laboratory of the Carnegie Institution of Washington facilitated marine biology studies out of its station on Loggerhead Key. Coral researchers, ornithologists, fish biologists, botanists, and other scientists visited the laboratory, conducted research, and spread word of the biological importance of the Dry Tortugas. The natural environment of the reefs and offshore waters continued to attract fishermen coming from Key West. Two such fishermen of note were Ernest Hemingway, who used his experiences at the Dry Tortugas to write a short story, "After the Storm," and Franklin D. Roosevelt, who as president was to play an important role in the fort's history a few years later.

Herbert K. Job's visit to the Dry Tortugas was important in their conservation history. He wrote about and, as importantly, photographed the Bird Key tern colony. Two of his images of sooty terns are shown. The Dry Tortugas were and are the only nesting site of this species in continental North America. Theodore Roosevelt was an admirer of Job's photography, which inspired Roosevelt's adding the Dry Tortugas to his coastal necklace of federal seabird reservations. The nesting island was patrolled seasonally by an Audubon warden into the 1930s. The birds shifted their nesting to Bush Key when Bird Key washed away in the 1930s. Within the continental United States, masked boobies and brown noddies also nested only on the Dry Tortugas and similarly were protected by Roosevelt's bird reservation. (Both, KH.)

Under protection, the sooty tern population built from a few thousand to 50,000–75,000 nesting annually. People interested in the unique seabirds of the Dry Tortugas made the journey to visit the nesting colony, watching for pelagic birds en route. These images of binocular-carrying visitors illustrate the adventure. Naturalist visitors included amateur bird watchers, biologists, and those interested in bird conservation. John B. Watson began experimental studies of the terns in 1907, early in the career of this soon-to-be-famous and controversial behaviorist. Birds he translocated to Cape Cod and the Yucatan had no problem finding their way back to the Tortugas. His objective, experimental approach used on the Tortugas was an important model for subsequent behavioral studies. (Both, MCPL.)

In 1905, the Carnegie Institution of Washington was convinced by Alfred G. Mayor to create an in-house marine lab and to put it on the Dry Tortugas. Mayor's Tortugas lineage ran deep as a mentee of Alexander Agassiz, son and scientific successor to Tortugas pioneer Louis Agassiz. Mayor built the Tortugas Laboratory on Loggerhead Key. Shown is Mayor on his first research vessel, *Physalia*. Mayor studied jellyfish and corals. (CIW.)

The main laboratory building, located on the north end of the island, was built in New York and then reassembled on the Tortugas. The station site included a dock, laboratory, bunkhouse, director's house, and kitchen. A cistern held fresh water. After the departure of the Navy's condenser, much of the fresh water had to be brought all the way from Key West, a logistical matter tended to weekly. (CIW.)

A windmill might seem out of place on an island without fresh water. This one, shown in 1911, provided flowing saltwater for the research aquaria. The aquarium lab was located in a building attached to the pier. Its sister building was the kitchen, built away from the other buildings for safety. The lighthouse is shown in the distance; the Loggerhead beach is in the foreground. (USGS.)

The laboratory contained workspaces for 14 visiting scientists. Scientists were invited for the short spring–summer research season and assigned a table and research space; over 150 scientists worked at the lab during its history. Scientists published hundreds of scientific papers from research at the laboratory, including 33 volumes of its own journal, *Papers from the Tortugas Laboratory of the Carnegie Institution of Washington.* (USGS.)

The stated focus of the Tortugas Laboratory was experimental research. This was an important distinction from the more observational natural history studies and species inventory explorations that had dominated science in previous decades. This image shows an array of jars in which to replicate experiments. (USGS.)

Despite the laboratory options, much of the research was done out on the reef, in the shallow water, and on the islands. Scientists had the use of various small boats from which to work. This image shows Arthur Sperry Pearse, who studied invertebrates. This Duke University professor was famous in the field for his biology, ecology, and parasitology textbooks issued for decades, beginning in 1917. (CIW.)

This is another view of the common laboratory showing workspace and a reference library, the maintenance of which in the damp and storms of the Tortugas was no doubt a challenge. Some of the invited scientists stayed only a short time, and others returned year after year to continue their research projects. (CIW.)

The director had a house, but others stayed in the bunkhouse (shown). Some of the distinguished scientists objected to such accommodations as well as a lack of family facilities. Food was another issue. One vocal food critic was geologist T. Wayland Vaughan, who brought his own food and also complained about the lab's biology focus. He then headed the competing, and nonbiological, Scripps Institution of Oceanography. (CIW.)

When the Navy could no longer provide logistical support, Mayor had the 70-foot research vessel *Anton Dohrn* constructed. It was named after the founding director of the world's first marine research station, Stazione Zoologica in Naples, Italy, the Tortugas Laboratory's model. The *Anton Dohrn* made weekly trips to Key West and also cruised to the Bahamas. Offseason, it went to Miami or took Mayor on distant research cruises. (CIW.)

Much of the research centered on the reef. A persistent question was coral reef growth, Louis Agassiz's question of a half century earlier. This 1910 image shows a "storm-proof" floating live car anchored off Loggerhead Key. Corals would be placed in the cages, where their growth could be measured under more controlled conditions. Mayor used them to compare the growth of various species, which he found to differ. (USGS.)

The Tortugas Laboratory made many pioneering advances in underwater studies. This image shows a scientist in a diving helmet and suit being assisted by a tender. The diving helmet had been in use for a hundred years, but its utility in biological research expanded at the Tortugas Laboratory. Before the invention of the on-demand regulator, free-flow diving helmets were the only way to access the reef bottom for long periods. (CIW.)

Another advance was underwater photography. Fish biologist William Harding Longley returned to the lab for 25 years, documenting 442 fish species. He developed the use of underwater photography to study fish as they actually appeared in their natural environment. He also pioneered the use of color underwater photography, which was celebrated in *National Geographic Magazine* in 1927. Longley became the laboratory's second director. (MDCPL.)

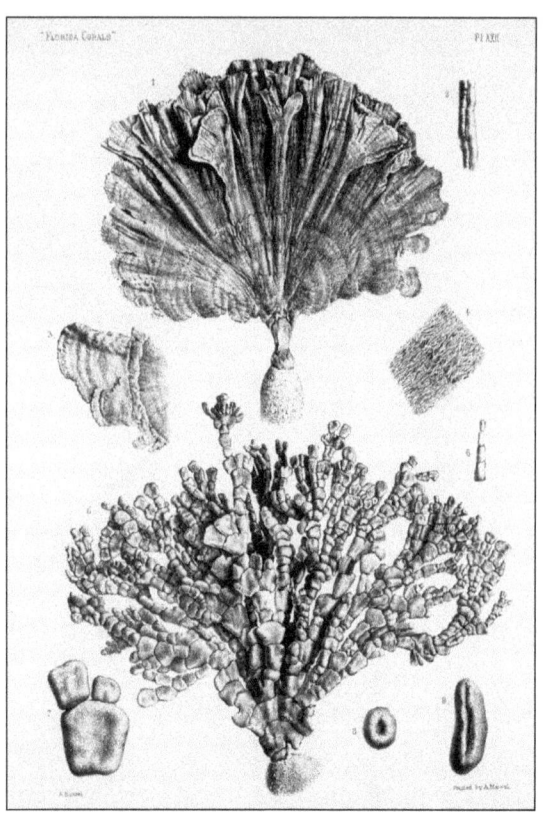

The origin of the Tortugas' sand was once warmly debated. The sand making up the islands and shallows, including the Quicksands, is not coral or shell but mostly algae, especially cactus algae, *Halimeda*. A coralline algae can multiply from 1 to 3,000 units in 125 days, providing an enormous amount of material to be pulverized into sand by wave action. This drawing is from Louis Agassiz's 1880 Florida Keys expedition. (NOAA.)

Another sort of Tortugas shore has elicited even more debate. Along Loggerhead Key, part of the shore is covered with beach rock, plates of calcium carbonate particles cemented together, its straight jointing looking human-made. The beach rock, which forms in place on the shore, has resisted the erosion shown on other islands. This image shows the shore in 1915. Today, the lower pipe has naturally been encased in stone. (USGS.)

Following Holder's Civil War–era observations, a study of the Tortugas' sharks was taken up by ichthyologist Eugene Willis Gudger. Gudger made exhaustive life history studies of various species, including the impressive and sometimes dangerous great barracuda. This is an image of a tiger shark he collected off Loggerhead Key in 1913. Recent research has shown that some sharks live their entire lives in the waters of the Dry Tortugas. (USGS.)

Generations of mariners, fort residents, soldiers, prisoners, lighthouse keepers, and Carnegie scientists brought in non-native plants to supplement the native vegetation, especially on Loggerhead Key. In time, these plants overran the island. One of Carnegie's visiting scientists, John Henry Davis, studied the vegetation, as documented in this 1939 image. Such information proved invaluable when the National Park Service later restored the vegetation. (SLAF.)

Although scientists of many interests passed through the Carnegie Tortugas Laboratory, the focus always returned to the coral reef. Studies of its geology, corals, fish, invertebrates, algae, and their physiological processes made the Tortugas reef the best understood in the world for its time. This image by W.H. Longley suggests the biological complexity that these scientists were unraveling. (MDCPL.)

Scientists were not the only ones collecting on the Dry Tortugas. The Tortugas Laboratory shared Loggerhead Key with the Coast Guard, who were tending the lighthouse. This picture shows an unidentified lighthouse staffer with his own coral specimen. Such collecting in the unregulated waters of the Dry Tortugas was probably not helpful to overall conservation and protection of the reef. (SLAF.)

Zane Grey had popularized fishing the Florida Keys internationally, and fishermen came to the Tortugas as well. Many focused on fishing the wrecks and reefs, catching groupers, snappers, mackerels, barracudas, and sharks. This photograph shows a goliath grouper at the government dock. Fishermen's catch helped document the reef's fish fauna. Others fished beyond the reefs in the Florida Strait, principally for billfish. (NPS.)

Ernest Hemingway visited the Dry Tortugas in his self-designed boat, *Pilar* (shown), to fish the Florida Strait, what he called in his books "the Stream." He was once stranded in the Tortugas for 17 days and knew them well. He spent part of 1934 fishing the Stream to assist scientists in characterizing then-confusing marlin species. Ernest Hemingway House & Museum commemorates his 1928–1940 residency in Key West. (MCPL.)

Mayor continued to lead the institution for 18 years, during which time the cream of American science accepted his invitation to spend part of the summer, resulting in enormous scientific productivity. Weakened by tuberculosis, Mayor died in an accident on Loggerhead Key in 1922. A monument was erected in 1924, shown with the buildings in the background. The laboratory continued under William Longley's leadership. (CIW.)

With weather, distance, logistical, and housing challenges, the Dry Tortugas were a difficult place to have a laboratory, as suggested by this image after the 1910 hurricane. Mayor himself was looking for a new site to expand into. After his death, Carnegie Institution's funding and the Tortugas' prioritization waned. Storms and a 1937 fire took out buildings. The lab closed in 1939; a few bits of ruins and Mayor's monument remain. (CIW.)

Six

A Place Far Apart

The 1920s and 1930s were difficult times for the Dry Tortugas' port city of Key West. The town went bankrupt. The Florida Emergency Relief administrator, Julius F. Stone, created the transformative goal to clean up and rebuild the city so as to turn it into a tourist destination. The plan succeeded. Over 40,000 visitors arrived during the 1934–1935 tourist season. It was then, in 1935, that Franklin Roosevelt declared Fort Jefferson and nearby waters to be a national monument. From that point, as part of the National Park System, the fort and its biological resources came under the protection and management of the National Park Service, which faced decades of neglect at the long-unfinished, long-decaying fort and the consequences of minimal oversight of marine resources. Visitors came from Key West to see the fort and experience swimming, diving, boating, camping, birding, and fishing adventures. After the closure of the Dry Tortugas Laboratory, scientific interests continued, especially in harvested resources, the reef, seabirds, and cultural resources.

Additional layers of official protection were added to the Dry Tortugas and nearby waters. In 1970, the fort was placed in the National Register of Historic Places. Congress affirmed the designation of the Dry Tortugas as a national monument in 1980 and in 1983 expanded its boundaries. In 1990, the Florida Keys National Marine Sanctuary was established to protect the coral reef and adjacent environments. On October 26, 1992, Dry Tortugas National Park was established by Congress and again enlarged, charging specifically that the historic cultural resources of Fort Jefferson and nearby waters were to be preserved and interpreted and the environmental values of the Dry Tortugas conserved. The federal and state governments had committed themselves to the importance of the heritage of the Dry Tortugas.

Given the degree of degradation, preservation of the fort and conservation of natural resources were to be major challenges. Better understanding of both cultural and natural resources led to new preservation and conservation measures. Native dune vegetation was restored on Loggerhead Key. Visitation increased, at the turn of the 21st century exceeding 80,000 people in one year, all of whom came by boat or seaplane. The Dry Tortugas passed the 500th anniversary of Juan Ponce de León's first landing, remaining a place of magic and inspiration, a place apart from the rest of the world.

By the early 1930s, the prosperous situation of the Dry Tortugas' neighboring port of Key West had changed. Military presence dwindled, the Great Depression inhibited tourism, and the 1935 hurricane tore up the train tracks, reisolating the lower Keys. Key West had lost nearly all of its industry, most of its jobs, and a third of its population and declared bankruptcy. This 1935 image shows a no-longer-thriving Key West. (SLAF.)

Among his initiatives, Florida Emergency Relief administrator Julius Stone established a camp on the Dry Tortugas. The workers cleaned, fixed, built, restored, and as this image from the 1930s shows, removed sand deposits from the moat. In 1935, up to 75 men were engaged salvaging the remaining metal. The fort was well in need of attention just as the National Park Service was being assigned to take over management. (NPS.)

Stone also engaged the Federal Art Project of the Works Progress Administration (WPA) in his plans, beautifying and publicizing the town by creating artworks and by establishing the Key West Community Art Center. Key West's WPA artists were sent to Fort Jefferson. One of these, F. Townsend Morgan, made this etching at the fort in 1935. It later became a popular tourist postcard. (MCPL.)

Having visited the Dry Tortugas islands in the 1920s as a private fisherman, Pres. Franklin D. Roosevelt's declaration of Fort Jefferson as a national monument was a personal remembrance of his own visit, a recognition of Theodore Roosevelt's declaration, and a complement to Stone's Key West revitalization. Roosevelt made a return visit to Key West in 1939 (shown) to inspect the progress of his New Deal policies there. (SLAF.)

The government took over the right-of-way of the hurricane-destroyed Florida East Coast Railways Key West Extension and built a continuation of the Overseas Highway, in places, as shown, directly on top. By 1938, the road was completed, and the Dry Tortugas again had a land route 70 miles away. Roosevelt's trip started in Miami and traveled the new road on his way to Key West. (MCPL.)

During World War II, the Key West military command assumed responsibility for southern defenses. Fort Jefferson's role was as a radar station and a seaplane base. Key West Harbor was home to minesweepers of the Inshore Patrol and escort vessels guarding against German submarines in the Florida Strait. Near war's end, in 1945, the Navy commissioned the first USS *Tortuga*. Shown here is the second USS *Tortuga*, commissioned in 1990. (NHHC.)

After the war, the new national monument began to take shape. It had been several decades since the Navy had given up responsibility for the fort and its ancillary facilities, and the fort's crumbling physical condition was to be one of the first challenges. South Florida began its postwar population boom while tourism resumed to the Dry Tortugas' fort and reefs. (NPS.)

Congress's 1992 redesignation of the Dry Tortugas as a national park was not just a name change. It provided additional expectations to understand, conserve, and interpret the fort, lighthouses, submerged cultural resources, reefs, fish, wildlife, and the islands. This image shows Chuck Pratt changing the well-known sign from Fort Jefferson National Monument to Dry Tortugas National Park. (Photograph by Eloise Pratt, ECP.)

The barracks structures had been undermined by salt air, hurricanes, the 1912 fire, and lack of maintenance. After study, they were determined to be too unsafe, and the above-ground structures were taken down in 1962. The beginning of the process is shown here. This initiative removed the fort's largest ancillary structures from within the parade. (NPS.)

The quarters' demolition produced a lot of bricks. Some were shipped to Key West; others were reused within the fort. This image from 1965 shows a walk around the parade being laid down using bricks recovered from the barracks. Other early enhancements included fixing the pier, restoration of cottages and casemate housing, and creation of interpretive displays. (NPS.)

The goal of stabilizing the fort was to preserve and interpret it as an outstanding example of a 19th-century masonry fortification. Fixing decaying masonry walls within the bounds of historic integrity was not an easy task. Research determined the most appropriate materials and methods. The formidable logistical issues facing craftsmen working in the Dry Tortugas needed to be overcome. These images show the degradation and how the restoration work proceeded, using both a floating platform from below and suspended platform from above. This stabilization initiative also presented the opportunity to create the replica shutters shown up close on page 37. (Both, NPS.)

A symbol of Fort Jefferson and the Dry Tortugas, the Garden Key light posed difficult conservation challenges as well. Like the shutters, the tower was made of iron and was subject to years of corrosion caused by the salty, damp, and hot marine environment. The light required repeated restoration efforts over the decades. This image shows restoration work being done in 1976. (NPS.)

Unlike the second Garden Key harbor light, the Loggerhead Key lighthouse was mostly brick and better withstood the elements. But metal components had corroded and had to be replaced with more weather-resistant stainless steel. Broken and missing windows, the copper roof, and the copper finial of the lightroom were also replaced. This image shows work on the roof panels. (NPS.)

Conservation of the remnant artillery pieces was a similarly complex task. The fort's Rodman and Parrot guns had lain corroding on the sand and coral fill of the terreplein for 100 years. They were restored and placed in position on replica carriages using a lift similar to what would have been available in the early 1900s. This 1982 image shows the work in progress. (NPS.)

Another extensive project was the restoration of the hotshot furnace. The furnace was studied forensically; it was disassembled three to five feet above its foundation; the iron components were refabricated in silicon-bronze alloy; and then the furnace was reassembled. The restored furnace is one of the features of the parade. (NPS.)

It has not been the intention to complete or totally restore the fort. The fort existed over a long period, changed with time and purpose, and was intentionally never completed. All such history is informative. Some ruins have been retained as such. The remaining supports for one of the coaling docks, shown in 1953, have provided generations of snorkelers an accessible way to see reef fish. (SLAF.)

The arches have always been an attraction. Cathedral-like in appearance and impact, they represent the finest of masonry fortification architecture, despite being constructed under some of the most difficult of conditions. What impresses a visitor most is not the degradation of the brickwork over time but the persistent integrity of the arches and the building they support. This image of tourist Jung-Hwan Na is from 1987. (HM.)

The natural environment also needed restoration. By the time of the park's establishment, most of Loggerhead Key had come to be covered with non-native plants such as coconuts, sisal, and Australian pines. Australian pines adversely affected sea turtle nesting. A project to restore Loggerhead Key's native dune vegetation and the dunes themselves started in 1995. Shown is a management burn removing non-native plants during the restoration work. (NPS.)

Preservation of cultural resources is difficult offshore. The number of wrecks in the park is not completely known, but by 1993, over 240 had been documented. There are certainly many more. Shown is the Windjammer site on Loggerhead Reef. The wreck, the iron-hulled three-masted ship *Avanti* built in 1875, has been a popular dive site. The previously mentioned Civil War–era Brick Wreck sank adjacent to the inner harbor. (NPS.)

Some of the stories occurred near but outside park boundaries. After 15 years of searching, Mel Fisher found the 1622 wrecks of the treasure-laden Spanish ships *Santa Margarita* and *Nuestra Señora de Atocha*. He found the *Atocha* debris field off the Marquesas in 1985. Its estimated worth was $450 million. Fisher had to defend ownership of his finds in court, in which he eventually prevailed. (SLAF.)

Fisher's salvage operations were dangerous, expensive, complicated, and endured their own shipwrecks. In 1975, his vessel *North Wind* sank, killing his son and daughter-in-law. Another, *Arbutus*, used as a bearing marker, sank in place on the Quicksands, shown in 1985. It remains visible on seaplane flights to the Dry Tortugas. Some of Fisher's recovered artifacts are on display at the Mel Fisher Maritime Museum in Key West (SLAF.)

There was other gold in Tortugas waters. Shrimp beds discovered off the Tortugas in 1947 started the "Pink Gold Rush." By 1951, about 19 million pounds of shrimp were harvested annually. The fleet of Key West shrimp boats put in at the Tortugas, shown in the 1950s. Stock depletion began by late 1950s; that, and farmed shrimp, ended the large-scale fishery by the late 1980s. Shrimp boats can still be seen on Stock Island. (NPS.)

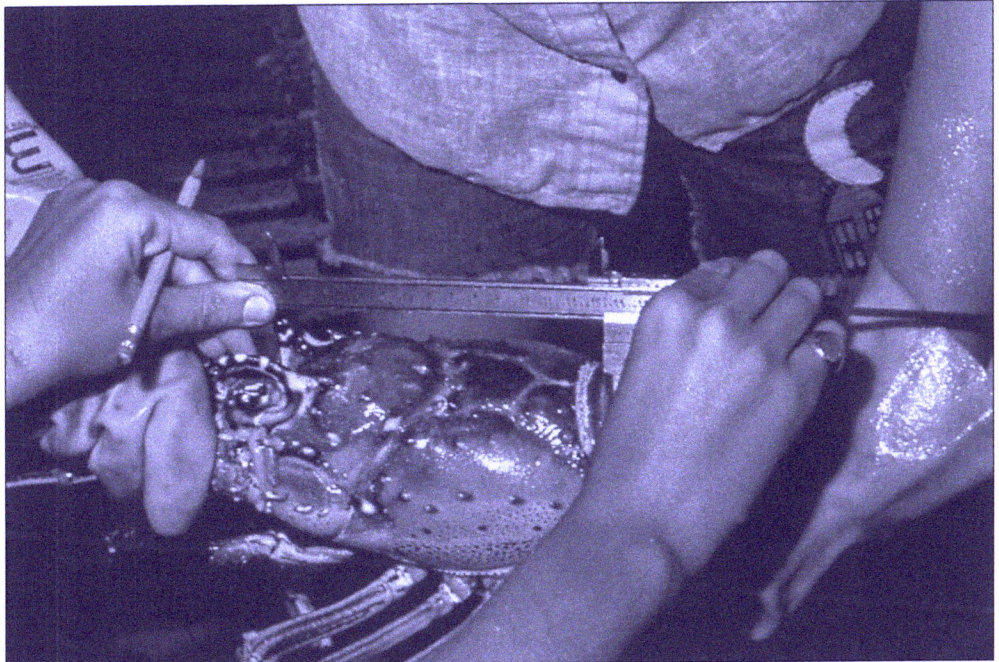

Another precious marine resource is spiny lobster. Studies in the 1970s led the park service and State of Florida to create a 47,000-acre lobster sanctuary. Spiny lobster have been protected in the park since that time. This 1980 image shows a lobster being measured. The Caribbean spiny lobster is a keystone species of the coral reef, maintaining its natural diversity. (NPS.)

In the early 1960s, the National Park Service began its own studies of the sooty terns that had put the Dry Tortugas on the radars of naturalists and conservationists such as Theodore Roosevelt. William B. Robertson Jr., shown here, began a long-term study during which over 500,000 sooty terns were banded. It is now known that Tortugas-nesting sooty terns spend off-season in the mid-Atlantic Ocean. (NPS.)

Despite protections, threats remain for Tortugas seabirds. Oil washed up on the Dry Tortugas in 1964 and 1970. This image shows cormorants caked with oil. Effects of the 2010 *Deepwater Horizon* spill in the Gulf of Mexico are still being studied. Boat groundings, which run the risk of an oil spill, were an important consideration in the 1989 Congressional designation of the Florida Keys National Marine Sanctuary. (NPS.)

During spring, birds migrating directly across the Gulf of Mexico or from Cuba towards their breeding grounds in North America end up landing on the Dry Tortugas. This migratory bird "fallout" at Fort Jefferson has drawn birders and ornithologists for decades. The image above shows the 1937 version of an annual trip sponsored by the Florida Audubon Society to see the migration and to band terns in the colony. The image below shows the senior author in 1970 during spring migration at the fort. Nearly 300 species of birds have been documented at the Dry Tortugas, with all but a few species being transient. (Above, TAS; below, KH.)

It was turtles that impressed Ponce de León in 1513, inspired his naming of the islands, and inspired mariners to come to stock up on sea turtles for food. Later, Key West's turtle soup industry caused the collapse of South Florida's green turtle population. Today, all species of sea turtles are considered endangered. Turtles use the reef, feed in the shallow grass beds, and nest on the islands. The image above shows men with a loggerhead turtle on Loggerhead Key in 1949. The image below, with Chuck and Eloise Pratt, shows a rarer leatherback turtle. Sea turtle nesting has been monitored in the park for decades, and East Key has been closed to visitors to protect that site. (Above, SLAF; below, ECP.)

Other species of concern make it to the Tortugas. Peregrine falcons follow the bird migration, continuing their hunt from the fort's walls and antennas. This image shows a West Indian manatee hanging out in the moat. An American crocodile lived at the moat for 14 years. Their origin is unknown. Manatees and crocodiles occur in South Florida and Cuba, equally distant from Fort Jefferson's moat. (Photograph by Eloise Pratt, ECP.)

As previously noted, the Tortugas are an important breeding and nursery area for sharks. The Nurse Shark Research Project has been studying them since 1991. This image shows Theo Pratt with a captured shark temporarily held in a kayak for processing. The Nurse Shark Special Protection Zone was established to provide security for mating and newborn nurse sharks. (NPS.)

Most visitors to Fort Jefferson come by boat, and by far most come by ferry. As early as the 1960s, the park service contracted with ferry operators to bring visitors to Fort Jefferson, leaving Key West in the morning and returning by the end of the day. Shown above is the high-speed catamaran *Yankee Freedom II*, predecessor to today's contractor boat *Yankee Freedom III*. Below are student passengers on an earlier ferry in 1970 napping their way back from the fort during an ornithology field trip led by University of Miami ornithology professor Oscar T. Owre. (Above, NPS; below, KH.)

Since their development, seaplanes have been a way to get to the Dry Tortugas; in World War I, Fort Jefferson was a seaplane base. This seaplane is pulled up onto the beach in the 1980s. Tourist flights have been provided by contractors, most recently by Key West Seaplane Adventures. Passengers have been able to see sand bars, reefs, sharks, rays, and Mel Fisher's sunken boat. (SLAF.)

In the early years of the monument, overnight visitors set themselves up for the night in the casemates, but to protect the fort, a camping area was created outside the fort walls. Visitors then could, and still can, spend a night or more at Garden Key's primitive camping area, shown in this 1999 photograph. (NPS.)

Much of the cultural history of the Dry Tortugas has remained hidden within crumbling brickwork, sand deposits, coral growth, and government archives. Little by little, historical and archeological research has revealed more and more. In this 1962 image, a ranger is photographed interpreting a cannon carriage to a young visitor. Interpretation of the fort was one of the expectations of Congress when the national park was established. (NPS.)

Over the decades, historical interpretation took many forms, including signage, establishing a museum, and tours by rangers and tour operators. This ranger is shown interpreting the plaque explaining the stay of Samuel Mudd. Stories of Dr. Mudd, the Conspirators, and the Civil War have intrigued visitors to the fort since the 1870s. (NPS.)

The pure white sand and coral beaches of the Dry Tortugas have also been attractions. On Garden Key, the main designated swim beach for decades has been a sloping shore on the island's southwest corner (shown). Bush Key beach has been open when the terns are away, and Loggerhead Key's long white-sand beach has provided a classic Caribbean feel. (NPS.)

Swimming using a face-plate (mask), breathing tube (snorkel), and fins developed in the late 1920s and early 1930s. Snorkeling's improvements over the next decades corresponded with increased visitor access to the Dry Tortugas, which provided convenient opportunities around the fort and on shallow reefs and wrecks where reef fish and other marine life have always been common. (NPS.)

Open-circuit self-contained underwater breathing apparatus, developed in the 1940s and 1950s, expanded into a recreational hobby, especially with improvements in wet suits, buoyancy compensation, and dive tables. Early scuba enthusiasts were able to explore the reef, characterized by large brain corals topped with branching staghorn coral, rather than the more usual elkhorn coral. The effects of ocean warming and disease are impacting coral, even in the Tortugas. (NPS.)

From before the days of Hemingway, the Tortugas' fish have drawn fishers from Key West. This 1979 image shows a typical snapper caught by visitor Jeff Beachum and unidentified boat mates. As boats and electronic aids increased, the overall sport fishery of the Florida Keys declined. From 1956 to 2007, the average fish size returned to the dock in the Keys has decreased from nearly 44 pounds to 5. (MCPL.)

Fort Jefferson has received some prominent visitors. In 1951, Pres. Harry S. Truman visited Fort Jefferson with an entourage for a tour and picnic. This image shows him in typical visitor posture, sitting on the fort floor. Adm. William Leahy is at left, and William Hassett stands to the right. The Little White House Museum in Key West commemorates Truman's winter residencies in Key West. (HTPL.)

Forty years later, another head of state visited. In 1991, England's Queen Elizabeth II stopped by the Dry Tortugas on her way from Miami to New Orleans on the royal yacht *Britannia*. She was greeted by Key West mayor Wilhelmina Harvey, who presented her with a conch shell, shown in this image, along with a certificate making her an honorary Conch before she and Prince Philip toured the fort. (MCPL.)

Being located directly north of Havana, the Dry Tortugas have been a destination for mariners from Cuba since the early 1500s. From the 1960s, refugees traveled from Cuba to the Dry Tortugas in all manner of small boats and other contrivances serving as boats, nicknamed "chuggs" for the sound of their motor, if they have one. The refugees, called *balseros* (originally meaning "raftsmen"), left their homes and risked their lives on the potentially dangerous trip, sailing, rowing, chugging, or being towed across the Florida Strait. During the Mariel boatlift of 1980, in less than six months, about 125,000 refugees reached Florida. The image above shows a refugee boat that arrived on Garden Key in 2000. The image below shows refugees adding to a thanksgiving memorial on Loggerhead Key. (Photographs by Eloise Pratt, ECP.)

The islands of the Dry Tortugas exist at the whim of tides and storms. There is no better illustration than contrasting what visitors might have experienced in different time periods. Historically, there was a channel separating Bush and Garden Keys. Navy ships of the line could come into harbor or to the coal docks. By the early 2000s, the channel had been filled in by storms forming a land bridge between the two islands. Bush Key also connected to Long Key. What were once three separate islands essentially became one. Future storms will continue to determine what Dry Tortugas islands are where. (Above, NPS; below, KH.)

It is now over 500 years since the Dry Tortugas were discovered and named by Europeans, over 170 years since Fort Jefferson's construction began, and several decades since the Dry Tortugas became a full-fledged national park. For centuries, mariners, army and navy forces, their prisoners, scientists, and adventuresome visitors, on approach, have seen the Dry Tortugas arise "as if by magic floating on top of the Gulf waters." Each day, visitors from Key West disembark at Fort Jefferson from the ferry, seaplanes, or private boats to be intrigued by the hulking fort, lighthouses, Dr. Mudd's story, tropical fish, the coral reef, and coral-overgrown wrecked ships. The front gates of the Civil War–era fort now stand open to receive them, as do the Caribbean-like waters. This image shows a 1996 Civil War–era reenactment of the fort's past. Each visitor cannot help but feel that past. Remote, historic, and surprisingly environmentally intact, the islands and waters of the Tortugas now find themselves protected within Dry Tortugas National Park. (NPS.)

Key to Courtesy Lines

CIW: Carnegie Institution of Washington
ECP: Eloise and Chuck Pratt Collection
HM: HistoryMiami Museum
HTPL: Harry Truman Presidential Library
JCBL: John Carter Brown Library
KH: Kushlan-Hines Collection
LOC: Library of Congress
MDCPL: Miami–Dade County Public Library
MCPL: Monroe County Public Library
MMA: Metropolitan Museum of Art
NHHC: US Naval History and Heritage Command
NLM: US National Library of Medicine
NM Nijks Museum
NMML: National Maritime Museum of London
NOAA: National Oceanic and Atmospheric Administration
NPS: National Park Service, South Florida Parks Collections Center and other sources
NYPL: New York Public Library
RM: Robert Marx
RP: Rawpixel
SBS: Eusko Ikaskutza–Society of Basque Studies
SLAF: State Library and Archives of Florida, Florida Memory
TAS: Tropical Audubon Society
UCL: University of California Libraries
UM: University of Miami Libraries Special Collections
UMA: University of Miami Department of Anthropology, Stock Island Collection
USCG: US Coast Guard
USGS: US Geological Survey Denver Library Photographic Collection
USNA: US National Archives
UTL: University of Toronto Libraries

Visit us at
arcadiapublishing.com